LOUISIANA SATURDAY NIGHT

LOUISIANA

Louisiana State University Press)|(Baton Rouge

SATURDAY NIGHT

LOOKING FOR A GOOD TIME IN SOUTH LOUISIANA'S JUKE JOINTS, HONKY-TONKS, AND DANCE HALLS

ALEX V. COOK

Published by Louisiana State University Press
Copyright © 2012 by Louisiana State University Press
All rights reserved
Manufactured in the United States of America
LSU Press Paperback Original
FIRST PRINTING

DESIGNER: Mandy McDonald Scallan
TYPEFACE: Minion Pro
PRINTER: McNaughton & Gunn
BINDER: Acme Bookbinding, Inc.

Unless otherwise noted, all photographs were taken by the author.

Library of Congress Cataloging-in-Publication Data

Cook, Alex V.
  Louisiana Saturday night : looking for a good time in south Louisiana's juke joints, honky-tonks, and dance halls / Alex V. Cook.
    p. cm.
  Includes index.
  ISBN 978-0-8071-4456-5 (pbk. : alk. paper) — ISBN 978-0-8071-4457-2 (epub) — ISBN 978-0-8071-4458-9 (mobi) — ISBN 978-0-8071-4459-6 (pdf)
  1. Dance halls—Louisiana—Guidebooks. 2. Music-halls—Louisiana—Guidebooks. 3. Bars (Drinking establishments) —Louisiana—Guidebooks. 4. Cajun music—Louisiana—Guidebooks. 5. Cooking, Cajun—Louisiana—Guidebooks. 6. Louisiana—Guidebooks. I. Title.
  GV1624.L68C66 2012
  725.8609763—dc23

                                                                        2011039036

To Jerri, you're the coolest

CONTENTS

NEW ORLEANS AND ENVIRONS

PREFACE

I had to drive all the way through town, past my own neighborhood, past the university and the strip malls that form Baton Rouge's exoskeleton, down the spinal column of Highland Road, past the Country Club and the big houses and whatever tony accessories that kind of life requires, past the water park, past the country homes, past, past, past. To get to the Alligator Bayou Bar I had to keep going past civilization and time itself. In the eighties, the Gator Bar was where you went on Sunday nights to escape Baton Rouge's archaic blue laws and party down with bikers, restaurant workers, and a raucous collection of drunks whose vehicles had gained a sort of autopilot home from the gravel road that got you to the tin building perched over the swamp. When I heard it reopened, I made a beeline to see if it was true. It had just snowed and the Saints were in the playoffs; anything was possible.

The road was built up. Alligator Bayou had been partially drained to accommodate the new neighborhoods that had sprung up in the decade since I'd been there, and there was nary a gator in sight. The owners had a tour business before the basin was drained profitable enough that they'd let the bar go dormant, but when that ran dry, they took the padlock off the door and gave it another go. Inside, the walls are a deep paneling tattooed up with a swamp scene and yellowed dollar bills stapled to the ceiling, fossils of many a night spilled out in the bar. A woman in sprayed-on jeans stood next to me at the bar getting another round; an old black dog named Floppy woke up to trail her vertiginous heels. A woman at the far end of the bar was crying, despite the earnest consolation of her date. A middle-aged woman kicked open the door and hollered, "Where's my Gator Bar?" and a weak cheer responded. There it was.

The band, a duo of vocalist and guitarist, was easing into their set and the crying girl was convulsively laughing. Somebody requested "Titties and Beer," and while the band professed, or maybe pretended, to not know that one, they gave Tears for Fears' "Everybody Wants to Rule the World" the Bonnie Raitt treatment and the room went aglow.

That glow turned out to be short lived. After a couple of weeks of dwindling crowds the bar went dark again, and I guess the only cars rattling down that road anymore are heading to multicar garages bringing the new denizens of the swamp to their couches and flat screens and into the fold of Greater America. There is nothing wrong with this per se. It appears to be the natural order of things; it's just that the south Louisiana I love doesn't follow the natural order.

In my south Louisiana, interstate highways knife across lakes and swamps for interminable distances, supported on endless matrices of concrete pillars. The southern edge of the state is consistently being reclaimed by the Gulf. It's not too uncommon to find people speaking French, resentful that they were ever forced to adopt English. The vagaries of this culture mutate from town to town. The swamp Cajuns are different from the prairie Cajuns. The music wrought on accordions and washboards pulls from different sources. My south Louisiana is a place where it is not uncommon to see a seventy-year-old lady out at the bar at one in the morning.

It is a place where the blues was born at Sunday picnics on its plantations, and that music propagated throughout the rest of the country and the world and then came back, creating a feedback loop of suffering and the joy of persistence against that suffering. It is a place where people cling to the music of generations past in the form of swamp pop, warping the fabric of race and time and region, making the culturally passé current and vibrant.

It is a place where, in zydeco clubs, black men dress like cowboys and play syncopated, self-defining amalgams of all of this on the aforementioned accordions and washboards. There are a lot of accordions in this book.

And then there is New Orleans.

Breaking down Louisiana culture into atomic parts is tricky because subcultures intermingle and mutate: black meets white, affluent meets impoverished, town meets country, Cajun meets Indian meets French and so on, and the place where those interactions can best be observed is on countless wooden dance floors and at smoky bars tucked away in neighborhoods, at the end of dark country roads, sometimes in the less savory and picturesque corners of the state. Race, class, and language barriers slide a little with the clockwork of blues, of Cajun two-step, of swamp pop, of jazz, of zydeco, and it is in those places that the truth of this strange land can be witnessed. Louisiana's nightclubs are not the places where we carve out our future but where we play out our present, often in the shadow of the past.

In writing about Louisiana (or any) culture, I have found that trying to fit this weird land and its weird people and food and music into any sort of paradigm, or trying to sort out a simple point to it all, is a fool's errand. The intention of this book, instead, is to provide a personal map of these places as they exist at the time of its writing, with one eye on the history of how these places and customs came to be and the other on the hot band tearing it up on stage. There is a fair share of analysis, sure, because south Louisiana is a place that begs it; some unlikely things work here while some normally evident things fail. Ultimately, this book is a celebration of Louisiana's extraordinary vernacular on any given Saturday night and an invitation to explore it that I hope you will see fit to accept.

So for every shuttered Gator Bar, I salute the beleaguered former owners and cast-adrift patrons. You did what you could. Herein lies a healthy sampling of the bars and dance halls and honky-tonks that remain open in defiance of the times and logic. The interbred multicultural threads of south Louisiana culture have no easy beginning or end, nor do they have an easily defined center; hence, this book is not a comprehensive listing of bars and clubs for the areas investigated. Rather, it is a staggering tour through many of the places I've found that make Louisiana nightlife unique. I start this journey where my own Louisiana music awakening took place, just north of Baton Rouge. But really, feel free to start anywhere in the book.

ACKNOWLEDGMENTS

A man who sets out to write a book about going to bars should first of all thank his loving family, for putting up with and encouraging the project. So above all, Jerri and Maya, thank you. None of this could have been done without your support.

Second on the list are James Fox-Smith, Dale Irvin, and the rest of the staff of *Country Roads* magazine for believing that I have something to say about these places for all these years. Much of the material found in this book had its gestation in my monthly column in that magazine's pages.

One must thank one's editor, Rand Dotson, for working with me and kicking me into gear when I needed it.

I want to shout out to my "research assistants," those who braved the dodgy directions and dark nights (and occasional early mornings) and the possibilities of the old bar having been shut down for years to risk having a good time in the unlikeliest of places. MVP among them is my buddy Clarke Gernon, as well as Chip and Annie Osbourne, Jeremiah Ariaz, Jerry Morgan, Andrea Hebert, and many others.

Special thanks to Frank McMains for letting me use his stunning photo of Teddy's Juke Joint on the cover.

Thanks to Arn Burkoff for maintaining the most comprehensive and up-to-date calendar of Cajun and zydeco events, originally called the Patsy Report and now titled the Louisiana Edition with Festivals. The website arnb.org is often the first place I check when plotting one of these adventures.

Also, thanks to all those who heard of this project through whatever grapevine or message board and suggested places I needed to see.

LOUISIANA SATURDAY NIGHT

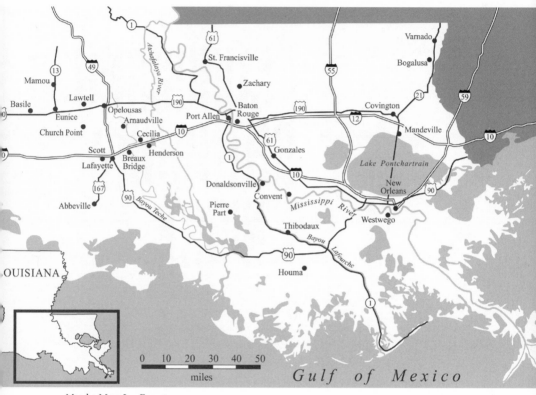

Map by Mary Lee Eggart

PROLOGUE

Teddy's Juke Joint

BACKWOODS BLUES CLUB WITH BANDS MOST FRIDAY AND SATURDAY NIGHTS, DJ SETS ON THURSDAYS

17001 Old Scenic Hwy.
Zachary, LA
70791
(225) 892-0064 or
(225) 658-8029
teddysjukejoint.com

I started out right here, then I went over there, and now I'm back up here!"

A sixty-one-year-old black man in a cape named Teddy Johnson bellowed that from the stage of his juke joint in Zachary, Louisiana. Underneath his cape, his red suit is obscured with money pinned all over it. The occasion is his sixty-first birthday party. On my party plate commingles a smothered turkey neck, a fried chicken wing, and the smeared remains of a piece of sheet cake. As I gnaw on the bones, Teddy relinquishes the microphone to the band, which lays right back into the groove as if the needle had been dropped.

Teddy's is the embodiment of "juke joint." The directions to get there are like a blues song: head up the fabled blues highway, Highway 61, north of Baton Rouge, turn down *old* Highway 61, go past the prison, and a mile down at the end of a gravel road you'll see a lone streetlight holding forth against the darkness. Down a long, gravel driveway lies this neon-festooned wonder. Teddy proclaims his to be the last juke joint on Highway 61, and he's likely right; there is just nothing else like this around anymore.

His exhortation from the stage can be read a number of ways. Primarily, he is referring to the fact that he was born in the house that serves as the juke joint, right where he stood on the bar's slightly elevated plywood stage. The "over there" is a dizzying tangle of holiday lights blinking in and out of sync, casting their erratic glow

Zachary

1

on an amalgam of bric-a-brac collected during Teddy's years as a DJ, spinning records in clubs with names like the Golden Rooster, Lizzie's Lounge, and the OJ Lounge. Holding court among all this is his massive DJ booth, adorned with teddy bears and an old "coloreds only" sign. The stage is "back up here," on stage at possibly the last juke joint in south Louisiana.

The ceiling is covered with so many strands of holiday lights it looks like a homemade version of the Las Vegas strip. The furnishings are a history lesson of long-gone clubs, as Teddy can tell you what defunct nightclub every barstool and knickknack came from. "I like lights and flashy stuff," says Teddy with a big smile. "I was brought up that you don't throw away nothin.'"

Teddy opened his club in 1979 after a stint as a house painter—the dry-erase board beside the front door boasts the self-applied sobriquet, "Your belly-rubbing, titty-sucking, nipple-squeezing painter man." Despite the brio in such a catchphrase, it was his mother who convinced him to start a place of his own. "I was doing record spinning, but I figured I could be making more money at my own place. My mother told me, 'There's this old house back there, why don't you make a club out of it?'"

Teddy's club spans the old and new definitions of a juke joint. "Juke joints are a symbol, a place where you can relax, listen to music, and just have a good time. Most places back then couldn't afford a band, so they would have a jukebox, or a guy spinning records." Teddy does this very thing every Thursday night and between band sets, often talking over the record, singing along, cracking jokes, or calling out to people in the bar. The playlist runs the gambit from bedroom R&B like Teddy Pendergrass, to Baton Rouge blues artists like the Neal family, to classics like Bobby "Blue" Bland and B.B. King. Like the smooth upscale blues Teddy favors and most Baton Rouge blues artists play, his juke joint, glimmering out there in the woods off Old Scenic Highway, is a rectification of the common preconception of the blues—feral music played by blacks out

Interior of Teddy's
Juke Joint

in the fringes of town—and the desire of African Americans to transcend that image.

Teddy kept the tradition of Sunday night blues jams—going back to the music's origin in plantation days, when black musicians would gather on the one night they had off work—alive as long as possible until the city shut down his Sunday night shows, but local, regional, and occasionally national blues acts find their way to this little glittering shack in the woods on Friday and Saturday nights. The real night to go, though, is Thursday evening, or any weekend night when Teddy doesn't have a band booked, in order to experience one of Teddy's DJ sets. He is Buddha in the lotus of his ornate DJ booth, his many-ringed fingers pulling from all tributaries of the blues, focusing mainly on slow jam R&B and "nasty songs," as one of my friends puts it. Teddy takes to the mic throughout the set in a stream-of-consciousness ramble of memories, shout-outs to people in the crowd, and bursts of self-promotion. Go there enough times that Teddy knows your name and he'll announce you when you enter the place, and you'll feel like Sinatra.

Teddy's wife, Nancy, runs the kitchen, dishing up soul food until late in the night, the rock around which Teddy orbits, peacock-strutting in a killer suit and, if the mood hits, a cape. "I got a pink crushed-velvet one, too, I wear on special occasions." The cape has links to the church, to royalty, to a personal sense of ascension. "When I stopped painting houses, I decided I was gonna start dressing nice all the time and that's where the cape came in."

The thing that surprised me most about Teddy's when I first

went there in 2006 is not that it was there but that I'd never heard of it. I've been on the periphery of the Baton Rouge blues scene for years, known a number of the musicians and fans, and I'd never heard it mentioned. It's only about fifteen minutes' drive from downtown Baton Rouge, but for most people in this sedentary town, it might well be on the moon. This book is intended to be a bridge to that moon, an invitation and a guide to those not-so-distant places in the Louisiana night that are unlike any others.

BATON ROUGE
and
SURROUNDING AREAS

Boudreaux & Thibodeaux's

CAJUN–THEMED MULTILEVEL BAR IN DOWNTOWN BATON ROUGE

214 Third St.
Baton Rouge, LA
70801
(225) 636-2442
bandtlive.com

Boudreaux & Thibodeaux's could be described as an attempt to create a Louisiana patina from scratch, utilizing a liberal mix of drink specials and Cajun kitsch. You leave the heat radiating off the concrete of downtown Baton Rouge with a blast of air-conditioning when you hit the door. Perhaps it is fitting that the bar is named for "Boudreaux & Thibodeaux" jokes, the generic Cajun stand-ins for the same jokes people make about other cultures—not that the bar mocks Cajun culture, but it accepts with humor the realities of Louisiana culture in the here and now.

Boudreaux & Thibodeaux's is one of the few venues in town that hosts zydeco acts, bringing in the wild yelps of Creole accordion cowboys to the white Bud Light set of Baton Rouge. You get the dancers twisting away on the floor when Travis Matte comes through town, but it is not the embrace of an identity that you see out in Opelousas. Zydeco becomes just another facet of the variety bands that dominate the music calendar here. With its balcony bar, it is not uncommon to find a southern rock band playing downstairs and a singer-songwriter upstairs. It's a reflection of what Louisiana has become culturally: a place that name-checks the details of the culture without fully engaging it. I'd love to see a full-time zydeco club in downtown Baton Rouge, but I doubt it would be able to stay open—so for Boudreaux & Thibodeaux's to latch on it at all makes me happy.

Boutin's

CAJUN RESTAURANT WITH DANCE FLOOR, LIVE CAJUN MUSIC EVERY NIGHT

8322 Bluebonnet Blvd.
Baton Rouge, LA
70810
(225) 819-9862
boutins.com

Cajun music fares a little better in the city. Boutin's Restaurant sits in the site of the old Mulate's, a satellite branch of the faded Breaux Bridge staple, fulfilling the duties asked of such an establishment: fried seafood on the menu and a well-maintained dance floor with 7 and 9 p.m. sets of live Cajun music every night it's open. Thursday through Saturday the second set starts at 10 and runs later, accommodating the Baton Rouge two-stepping nightcrawler. Boutin's gets a respectable crowd for its reliable cycle of artists like Lee Benoit, Mel Chavis, Coobie Joe, Al Berard, and Jay Cormier. The ample restaurant and access to the interstate as well as its inviting atmosphere set it up well for tour groups, a plus given the relative remoteness of some of the other dance halls in this book.

Boutin's is a one-stop shop for Cajun immersion. Not only are the walls festooned with George Rodrigue's "Blue Dog" paintings, swamp scenes, and folk art signs, but the restaurant has partnered with Poche's Meat Market from Breaux Bridge, allowing it to open a Cajun mini-mart in one corner of the establishment. There are not too many places one would suggest bringing your appetite, your dancing shoes, and an ice chest for the ride home. All they need is a canal and a boat launch (though Bluebonnet Swamp Nature Center is just down the street), and it would be a complete package.

Chelsea's Café

LAID-BACK RESTAURANT, BAR, AND VENUE; ROOTS ROCK, CAJUN, AND R&B BANDS
THURSDAY THROUGH FRIDAY

2857 Perkins Rd.
Baton Rouge, LA
70808
(225) 387-3679
chelseascafe.com

Another club that has edged its way into Baton Rouge's social identity is Chelsea's. Chelsea's goes for a broader approach: it's a restaurant with an ambitious menu yet a bar-and-grill atmosphere; it has a back patio and a side bar a hallway away from the stage area, where a litany of regional and touring, predominantly roots-oriented bands with a nod toward Cajun, zydeco, and New Orleans brass bands and funk draw the college-age and post–college-age crowd. When the bar was almost shut down in 2009 because of licensing disputes, a group of patrons packed the courtroom for the hearings. To them, and to many others, Chelsea's is home base, a laid-back respite from the rest of the city determined to put in as many chain stores and restaurants as it can.

Chelsea's defies Baton Rouge's inclination for homogenization by blurring the edge between suburban acquiescence and the vagaries that a drunken night can hold. One evening I witnessed the Pine Leaf Boys, one of Lafayette's best young Cajun groups, tear through a thundering set of waltzes and two-steps with a bit of bewilderment about them; no one was dancing. There was a spot-lit vacuum on the floor between the band and the young college crowd lurking in the bar's shadows. Eventually, one young couple broke the seal, and within a song or two, the rest of the room followed and the room was awhirl. Soon the frat guys shouting over a pool game in the front bar and the smokers from the patio joined in the fray. It wasn't the synchronized display of cultural reverence that you get in Acadiana dance halls or the congenial abandon that you find in New Orleans, but it was a chink in the dam. I love Chelsea's for that. It does for Baton Rouge's uptight clientele what Louisiana does for the rest of the country; it gets folks to loosen up a bit.

DETOUR:

Buddy Stewart's Rock Shop and the Rhythm Museum

1706 North Acadian Thwy.
Baton Rouge, LA
70802
(225) 383-9661

I found out about the first stop in this book, Teddy's Juke Joint, from a faded flyer tacked to the door of Buddy Stewart's Rock Shop, a glorious old-school record store standing on a strip of Acadian Thruway that in the sixties and seventies bustled with R&B clubs. Like Teddy's, the Rock Shop is a final vestige of a past I thought long faded. While the owner, Philiper Stewart, took a phone call, I fell into the natural pose in which much of my college years were spent: fingers out, flipping through albums. Flap, flap, flap, flap . . . I love that sound almost as much as the music on them.

Philiper explains that the Rock Shop has had to make some adjustments to its business model to stay afloat over the years and is in the process of becoming the Buddy Stewart Music Library. "We find that people walking in the door are more interested in researching the history than purchasing the records. Some still do purchase records, and we appreciate when they come through, but we can't rely on that business to keep the doors open." Two cubicles on one side of the room house a seasonal tax preparer's office, and Philiper's son Dell runs a barber shop next door.

In those stacks of records, the loose story of Baton Rouge blues starts to come together. Buddy Stewart was a saxophonist and big-band leader in the fifties and sixties, taking his Top Notches around the South and leading the Herculoids, a backup band for performers like Solomon Burke and Jackie Wilson when they came through in the 1960s and 1970s. Stewart wrote regional hits with Chuck Mitchell ("Your Precious Love") and Gene Fairchild ("Another Shoulder to Cry On") as well as "If I Ever" with vocalist Lee Tillman under his own name on the Ron label. Stewart opened his record shop on Thirty-third Street, before it was called Acadian Thruway, in the sixties, when it was the blues avenue in Baton Rouge. "Everywhere you see a church up on this street, there was a juke joint or a nightclub," says Philiper, who took over the business in 1997 and has maintained her father's legacy ever since. Philiper echoes the money problems one inevitably hears in relics like this, but her one concern is keeping the doors open and the history alive. "I would love the museum next door to really become that—a permanent museum where people can relive this music and see where we came from."

The Rhythm Museum is a large rental hall that used to host a spectacular Monday night R&B jam and is home base for music education classes for kids, but the real draw is the staggering grid of photos from Baton Rouge's blues past, all staring back with that particular press photo smile. Along the north wall are exhibits in glass vitrines, almost like projects at a special blues-themed social studies fair, artifacts like Stewart's old records with the Herculoids, so-and-so's guitar, displays honoring the blues patriarch Raful Neal and his daughter Jackie.

Among the artifacts is a 1961 Arhoolie-label collection bluntly titled *Country Negro Jam Session,* composed of field recordings made by Dr. Harry Oster, an LSU English professor who started documenting black musicians in the area in the 1950s. Notable among them is Zachary blues guitarist Robert Pete Williams, captured on tape while incarcerated at Angola prison, a place Oster described in his 1969 book *Living Country Blues* as "enclosing some three thousand caged and womanless Negroes . . . a fertile breeding ground for the blues." Williams, a farm worker being held for killing a man in a bar fight, evinces in Dr. Oster's recordings a timeless suffering, an epitome of the country blues where a ramble of lyrics, sometimes plainly spoken rather than sung, rests over an almost disembodied drone on the guitar, as if the music is a train and the singer merely a rider. He is like a fly lamenting his state in the web.

Another find by Dr. Oster is the fiddle music of Butch (James) Cage, born in 1894 outside Meadville, Mississippi, but retired in the north Baton Rouge neighborhood of Scotlandville, playing a long-forgotten form of fiddle music for backyard parties. Dr. Oster was following in the footsteps of Alan Lomax in attempting to document a fading cultural heritage in the context of the times, and thus, through these recordings, we follow in his.

Buddy Stewart's Rock Shop, once a treasure trove of lost forgotten blues, has been picked over by collectors making treks through the area and, like many of the steps on the blues trail, is in danger of being weathered away.

In *Living Country Blues,* Dr. Oster lays out the differences between "country blues and city blues": "spontaneous expressions of thought and mood" versus "planned arranged texts and music," and "fluid use of form" versus "precise classical form, predictable twelve-bar structure." This supposed conflict is, in my mind, duked out continually between blues aficionados and blues fans. The aficionados long to hear Robert Johnson or Charley Patton coaxing the devil's music out of ramshackle acoustic guitars at even more ramshackle places, and really, who could blame them? That music speaks to a primal longing that lies dormant in all of us, an internal mangy dog that usually cowers under the porch of modern life, venturing out to address the moon. This is what the blues aficionado seeks, and unfortunately, it pretty much doesn't exist in the wild anymore. Even back in Harry Oster's time, eager blues enthusiasts were scouring courthouse records and old-folks homes for the real country bluesmen to buffet the folk revival of the sixties, and it is in that curated heritage that the blues aficionado seeks the greater truth of this dwindling art.

Interior, Buddy Stewart's Rock Shop

Phil Brady's

CITY BLUES DIVE, BANDS FRIDAY AND SATURDAY NIGHTS, BLUES JAM ON THURSDAY EVENINGS

4848 Government St.
Baton Rouge, LA
70806
(225) 927-3786
philbradys.org

Phil Brady's sits in an unassuming strip of businesses on Government Street, staggering distance from this author's house, and it is the kind of bar you want within that range. To cast it as a dive would be a bit of a betrayal, for it doesn't really embrace that sort of glowing dive patina, but it is dive-y. Its clientele skews older and, like the club, has generally seen better days yet chooses to embrace the here and now of Baton Rouge's cultural lifeblood, the blues. Phil Brady's has been hosting its Thursday night blues jams since time immemorial, each night hosted by one of the city's guitar- or harmonica-wielding stars. More often than not, a steady band congeals around the old players as they revisit sweet home Chicago and call out "Big Boss Man" like they've done for years.

The real beauty, though, is when the unexpected happens. I can remember one blues jam in the late nineties when the regular guys were approached by an excited kid bedecked in denim and a wide smile. He was from Russia, touring the South looking for America without a real grasp on the specifics. The guys in the band were doing their best to understand the kid and figure out what he could play on the spare guitar at which he pointed; one guy in the band jokingly asked if he knew "Back in the U.S.S.R." He shrieked, "YES!" and they pulled him up on stage. You could see this kid's smile all the way from those Ural Mountains way down south, playing on a stage with real blues musicians. The group tried to coach him through a couple of blues numbers with stumbling results, and at a blues jam, stumbling makes the natives restless. This went on for two or three songs, wearing thin the

Entrance, Phil Brady's

perestroika his enthusiasm had brought until somebody shrugged, "What the hell, let's do it again," and they launched back into "Back in the U.S.S.R." The bar erupted in applause, perhaps because it heralded the end of the Russian kid's set. It didn't matter; he left the stage a star.

Another guy I've wondered about is Stanley. On another blues jam night, a skinny man still in work clothes took the mic and addressed the crowd with a nasal twang. "Hi, I'm Stanley and I work at a plant in Port Allen." Stanley then launched into the most heartfelt version of Larry Williams's "Bony Maronie" anyone has possibly ever played. He did a few other blues numbers with similar gusto, pulled out a harmonica at one point, if memory serves, but his "Bony Maronie" will stay with me forever, which is just as well, because after a few songs he stepped off the stage and out the door never to be seen again.

This is blues-fan blues, the kind that has its roots in the authentic but ultimately is more concerned with a good time and, despite the lamentations of blues aficionados, holds a more palpable tie to the beloved blues tradition than does the folk revival style. Those Sunday fish fries, those prison rambles, those freight train exultations were primarily about entertainment in defiance of a cruel, crushing world. The blues exists today not because it is pure—there was nothing ever really pure about it— but because it spoke and continues to speak in the grand commonalities of love, loss, and libation, things that touch the heart beating beneath both a prison uniform and a Hawaiian shirt.

Tabby's Blues Box

Many in Louisiana would likely argue that Baton Rouge is one of the least Louisiana places in south Louisiana—and a terrible place to start exploring the state. The capital city, it skews more conservative than much of the surrounding area and seems to have a lower investment in its history. When Tabby's Blues Box moved from its original location by the train tracks to a downtown site because of the construction of an overpass, it had a hard time staying afloat. The old Tabby's opened in 1979 and, like Teddy's Juke Joint, was a place you couldn't believe existed. Everyone played Tabby's—Silas Hogan, Henry Gray (former piano player for Howlin' Wolf), Baton Rouge blues patriarch Raful Neal and his celebrated sons Kenny and Lil' Ray Neal all cut their teeth at Tabby's. Not to mention Tabby's own son Chris Thomas King, a singer celebrated for his efforts to push the blues into popular music contexts and an actor who found worldwide acclaim portraying Tommy Johnson in the 2000 Coen brothers film *O Brother, Where Art Thou?* It was also at Tabby's Thursday night Hoodoo Party blues jams that college students like myself, lured by less-than-stringent ID checks, got a taste for the blues.

Rockin' Tabby Thomas doled out the swamp blues from the stage and canned beer from an ice chest in the back and was a key aspect of the Baton Rouge blues identity. One night, I got my first taste of chitlins from the buffet as my roommates' band was trying out to be Tabby's new backup band for a European jaunt. The night, like my stomach after the chitlins, was unsteady, felt on the verge of collapse. Tabby just wasn't gelling with the band, and a détente was reached when Lil' Jimmy Reed, who happened to be in the room, was called to the stage to show 'em how it's done.

A blues prodigy from early on, Leon Atkins got the name

Lil' Jimmy Reed in 1957 when one night he went to see his hero Jimmy Reed perform at an upscale club. The fabled bluesman was too drunk to perform before the packed house. The promoters had seen Atkins perform and knew he knew every Jimmy Reed song by heart, so they put him on in Jimmy's stead. That night at Tabby's, he injected his turbocharged guitar artistry into the swamp blues set and saved the night, with my roommates hanging on for dear life. Then Reed looked out and said, "We're gonna call ol' Warren from Hardwood to sing one for the ladies." No one knows who Warren might be besides someone Reed knew from growing up in the small town near the Mississippi line on Highway 61, but ol' Warren tore into a set of Otis Redding and Johnny Adams tunes, knocked everybody out, and then disappeared, just like Stanley did that night at Phil Brady's. It might have been the chitlins and all the cheap beer working in alchemical consort, but that was the night my ears were opened to the blues, and every return visit to Tabby's only confirmed my belief that something unique and natural happened in that ramshackle club.

In 2000, the Blues Box moved to Lafayette Street downtown because of the overpass construction, and the new location never really took. Four years later, as Tabby was waiting to take the stage, he suffered a stroke, and soon after that the bar closed for good. At the time of this writing Tabby still gets out and sings every once in a while, and his popular radio show still airs every Sunday on WBRH, but Tabby Thomas exists as a warning that this blues history, along with Louisiana music history in general, is but a few incidents away from dissipating into memory. It's hard to find a place with ties to Louisiana culture that really works in a city like Baton Rouge, where the two dominant forces are LSU football and white flight to the suburbs and where, for ages, the art deco corridors of downtown Baton Rouge were lonely canyons. Fortunately, that is starting to change.

Floyd's Morley Marina

HOMEY MARINA BAR IN THE BACKMOST PART OF "BACK BRUSLY"

7675 Choctaw Rd.
Brusly, LA
70719
(225) 749-9640

Just like people, towns are born and towns die. In 1907, Horatio Throop Morley left his comfortable lifestyle in Michigan to carve out a new life and a new enterprise in the swamp six miles west of Brusly in West Baton Rouge Parish. He gave birth to a community that would bear his name and the community of Morley would thrive for nearly twenty years, surviving just slightly longer than its namesake." So opens an uncredited essay fronting a packet of material about the lost town of Morley, handed to me by Floyd Prejean on the back porch of the Morley Marina, a bar Prejean has owned for eighteen years down at the dead end of Choctaw Road in Brusly. The story has it that "H. T. Morley turned down an offer in 1915 from a then penniless friend in Michigan, Henry Ford, to join him as an investor in his struggling car company."

Horatio and his brother Lawrence instead made a significant amount of money—$7 million—in the cypress logging enterprise out in what is now known as "Back Brusly," on 17,000 acres that their father ("a carpetbagger," states the article) acquired during Reconstruction. Among the documents in Mr. Prejean's dossier is a listing of the holdings of the Morley Cypress Company, including:

> One complete band saw mill, with nine
> foot band saw, in fine running order
> 25 dwellings for white laborers in white town
> 107 homes in negro town
> One large store
> One ice house
> One dance hall

Morley's old friend Ford was finding his own success in the automotive business and sent the Morleys a gift of a Model T by barge. Morley fitted it with large tires so he could drive it on the muddy road around his logging empire in Back Brusly. In 1923, however, Morley met his end on River Road, on his way back from the Baton Rouge Country Club with his uncle-in-law, George Coswell. Morley was at the wheel of his preferred ride, a Stutz Bearcat.

"A Nash Rambler honked to pass," a newspaper article by Richard Boudreaux in Mr. Prejean's file puts it, "but Morley, determined to stay ahead in any endeavor, gunned the engine. His wheels caught loose wet gravel on the shoulder and the car plunged into a ditch killing the two men."

The cypress was largely all cut down by then, and though the company had other hardwood interests to keep it afloat, without Morley at the helm the enterprise shortly withered, as did the town.

The weekend I visited, the marina seemed pretty busy for a dead town. Morley Marina lies on the Intracoastal Canal next to one of the only public boat launches in West Baton Rouge Parish. It was the Sunday before July 4, and I could hear the low murmur of water-skiers mixing with the braggadocio of fishermen, the occasional firecracker popping against the dull roar of an impending storm, the sudden chorus of the Emergency Broadcast System erupting from every boat radio. This is a place for regulars. In fact, if you aren't a regular, chances are you've never even heard of the place. An old man clapped me on the back as I watched a guy try to winch his boat onto a trailer on the launch just as a water-logged dog splashed in next to him after a stick. "Welcome to Brusly Paradise," the guy laughed. The bar is open seven days a week, starting around noon and winding down around dark, but the night to go is Sunday when a cycle of variety bands plays.

Prejean stood with me on the back porch and pointed to the tugboat-repair facility just to the south on the Intracoastal.

Back porch at Floyd's
Morley Marina

There, in 1955, Lawrence Morley's grandson Morley Morgana built the original marina from the bricks of the old sawmill.

"They had a dance hall and a restaurant, and it was lined up with houseboats and yachts all along here," Prejean said, gesturing to the placid waterway. But the dredging of the waterway as part of the Intracoastal Canal killed that particular Morley enterprise.

"When the tugboats started coming through, they would make such a wake that all those nice boats would scrape the bottom, so they all left," said Prejean. With amazing narrative timing, the lazy calm of the marina was suddenly interrupted by a closely passing barge pushed by a massive tugboat, slogging their way down the canal.

An article from a 1976 issue of the West Baton Rouge *Chronicle* states, "Finally in 1964, the family sold the last parcel of land, thus removing even their name 'Morley' from future maps."

As the late summer sun set over the woods in which H. T. Morley found his fortune, the band L.A. 1 was deep in their set of classic R&B and the dance floor was packed with retirees swinging away to "Sweet Home Chicago" and the like. The Marina bar attracts mainly an older crowd of seasoned partiers. Wading through the crowd, I overheard one woman confide over the music to her friend, "I didn't bring no money, but one of these old boys'll buy me a drink." And sure enough, one of them did. The younger folks tend to gather on the porch after a day on the water, their fish stories getting louder with each beer ordered through a little window to the bar.

None of us drinking beers on the porch envied the effort expended by the guys trying to line their boats up on trailers

FLOYD'S MORLEY MARINA

at the ramp with a mildly drunken audience. But soon enough, each would give the high sign, the truck would peel out a little, and the boat would get parked yards away in the gravel lot as another would take its place.

A massive box fan at one end of the porch was a suitable substitute for the lack of a breeze out here in the backest part of Back Brusly, yet another unexpected perfect spot to catch the last gasp of the weekend.

Hymel's Seafood Restaurant

FAMILY-STYLE CAJUN RESTAURANT WITH LIVE CAJUN AND COUNTRY OPEN-MIC JAM ON THURSDAY AND SATURDAY NIGHTS

8740 La. Hwy. 44
Convent, LA
70723
(225) 562-9910

All expecting parents are deluged with advice as the time narrows between the abstract and concrete states of parenthood, but the best advice I remember from that fevered time was, "Your child must adapt to your life, not the other way around." It's a little simplistic and not precisely actionable, but it's something we have always kept in mind about raising our daughter, and partially because of it, she has been my best partner in crime for the past seven years. So when it was time to check out the music at Hymel's, the venerable River Road seafood restaurant in Convent, I figured why not indoctrinate her into this part of my life?

She has her own particular ear for music: any time a sweet melody should emerge from the car stereo, her first question is to ask if it's on a CD so we can listen to it again. I got her a copy of the Dixie Chicks' *Taking the Long Way* for the little jambox in her room, and within a week she was belting out her own heartbreaking version of their tribute to independence "The Long Way Around," chirping "but I, I could never follow" with a sense of pitch better than any she could have gotten from me. The promise of a real live country band plus what was rumored to be the best catfish in the area were enough to get her to sign on.

The instant we passed through the glass door to the lounge attached to the restaurant, we were confronted with the band, a circle of men on guitars, bass, and fiddle cycling through the country standards I'd grown up hearing. We were seated as they went through what I am pretty sure was an instrumental version of Lefty Frizell's 1950 hit "If You Got the Money (I Got the Time)."

Hymel's is the kind of restaurant that I wish was still the standard for family dining. A crowd of Formica tables each

Convent

Jam session at
Hymel's

covered with paper, plastic baskets of crackers, homey décor, and nary a cartoonish mascot in sight. The band continued its greatest hits of yesteryear at the perfect volume: loud enough to be easily heard, but low enough to talk over. I asked my daughter what she thought of this place, and she took a look at the platters of boiled shrimp being shuffled around and the plastic crawfish attached to one wall and said, "I like it. It looks Cajun-ish to me."

The food matched the décor—comforting and unpretentious. The seafood gumbo recommended by the waitress was a mildly seasoned yet pleasingly complicated thick concoction that mirrored the clientele. Young and old, families and young couples, kids and men just off their shifts at the plants nearby—all corralled together by the sound of the fiddle and harmonica and that familiar lope of Nashville's golden era.

Our food arrived in short order, considering how packed the place was, the canned soft drinks accompanied by small glasses. Pouring half a can of Coke into a glass may not seem like much at first, but comparing it with the assembly line ambience that usually accompanies eating with children, it was positively genteel. The catfish lived up to the reputation—thick filets in cornmeal batter fried to just the perfect degree—and the shrimp and oysters were perfectly crunchy. I'm fairly certain my daughter ate her first oyster as she was distracted by the sudden change in the music from the other room. The homey lope had suddenly taken on a Native American cadence, complete with the harmonica and fiddle playing the war cries. She looked at me with a quizzical look as the patrons in the bar began to clap along and the powwow turned into Hank Williams's "Kaw-Liga." I told her the song was about a statue of

an Indian that fell in love with another statue in a store across the street, but because he was made of wood, he could never go and talk to her. And then one day, someone bought the girl statue and he was sad that he had never gone to talk to her. She said, "So it's like he was shy," cutting through any metaphors of wooden hearts and hesitation.

We wolfed down our desserts and made it up to the front to watch the band sway through Ernest Tubb's "Waltz across Texas." By that time, the chord progressions had already ingrained themselves in my daughter's head; she was humming along with the song as we walked out the door. That is the beautiful thing about country music and family restaurants—to really do them right, they don't need to be updated or augmented or marketed to you. They just need to be allowed to exist, and thankfully Hymel's is still around to offer both a home.

Grace's Lounge

MODERN BAR FEATURING TRADITIONAL SWAMP POP BANDS

43435 Weber City Rd.
Gonzales, LA
70737
(225) 647-2047
www.graceslounge.net

Of all the strains of music that inform the Louisiana land-scape, swamp pop is the most difficult for me to pin down because in practice and in spirit it is the most common music there is, anywhere: oldies. It is composed of songs that everybody knows, that everybody's parents know, performed in the most reverential manner possible. It is *Happy Days* music to the rock 'n' roll of Fats Domino that weathers the storm of musical trends. It is possibly the least hip music there is—white-guy, Hawaiian-shirt, tourist-bar music. Yet in pockets of Louisiana, particularly out in Gonzales, there are musicians who transcend that indictment and fans who rise up to meet it.

I headed out to Grace's Lounge to see Foret Tradition, widely considered to be the best swamp pop band going. I pulled into the parking lot, struck by the lack of a big sign with a logo; there was just a rented sign that listed Foret Tradition and a number of regional rock acts. This did not bode well for pin-ning down a Unified Theory of Swamp Pop.

"Well, you know when you hear music from New Orleans, and you know what it is?" said Grace's manager, Brandon Moran. "Swamp pop is like that. It's music from the fifties and sixties dance bands with a local flair." First opened in 1974 by Grace Vasseur, the club has always operated as a live-music venue. Moran books a variety of music, reflecting the chang-ing face of Ascension Parish, but Thursday nights are all for swamp pop. "I grew up in a house where my parents danced to swamp pop," he explains, listing Mike Broussard & the Night Train Band, Kane Glaze, and the Coozan Band as some of his parents' favorites.

Foret Tradition kicked into their horn-laden upgrade of bar-band classic "Mustang Sally," James Spells's trumpet and Ryan Foret's soulful growl injecting some of the

Gonzales

Foret Tradition at
Grace's Lounge

Wilson Pickett swing into the song that has been worn down by a million bad variety band covers. The women in the bar dropped every conversation and margarita glass to break into one of the most spontaneous line dances I've ever seen. As the song blazed on, I started to see some defining edges to this thing called swamp pop. It wasn't about the songs themselves; it was about how and where it's played. Foret Tradition tore through classics like "Domino" with an injection of Crescent City funk and blare from the horns, making these old songs rise like a wave only to crash when they reach their fever pitch.

The most defining characteristic of swamp pop, though, is whom it is being played for. The Forets' rendition of Slim Harpo's classic "Ti-Na-Ni-Na-Nu" set the checkered floor into a jitterbugging frenzy, couples flinging and twirling in every direction. I'm used to seeing older couples demonstrate how a rug gets cut at Cajun dance halls, but I was shocked to see how well the younger people in the crowd knew the steps.

I approached two young women in their twenties as they exited one of the evening's many synchronized Electric Slides. They appeared to be about nineteen, though I supposed their IDs said different. I asked them why two young women were so into a batch of songs nearly a half century old. One blurted without hesitation, "This is my kind of music. I was born and raised here and this is what we listen to."

When I asked whether they practiced the dance steps, her friend offered, "No way. I learned them from growing up here." I sensed indoctrination was at play—perhaps they were members of the extended Foret family. My last shred of skepticism about how ingrained this music was in the youth culture here dissipated when I asked the crucial question in identifying the true teenager, "OK, but what CD is in your car stereo right now?" And they responded by pointing to the band and saying in unison, "THIS ONE!" They quickly disappeared into yet another flurry of twirling bodies, leaving me to realize that I may still not know what swamp pop is exactly, but I have a good idea of who and where it is.

Swamp Pop Festival

Lamar-Dixon Expo Center
9039 S. St. Landry Ave.
Gonzales, LA
70737
(225) 621-1700
swamppopmusicfest.com

Back behind the Cabela's that holds court with the outlet mall along I-10 in Gonzales lies the massive Lamar-Dixon Expo Center. It's the site of 4-H fairs and motorcycle rallies, but twice a year it becomes an embodiment of the strong embrace this area has on swamp pop. In November it hosts the Festival of Festivals, sort of a trade expo of Louisiana's many regional festivals, and in June, the Swamp Pop Festival. The building is fitted with thousands of folding chairs, and jambalaya and beer vendors are at the ready as Gonzales becomes the center of the swamp pop universe.

All the big shots are there: Foret Tradition, Warren Storm, Tommy McClain, GG Shinn, and so on playing to a packed dance floor twisting away under a massive mirror ball. At places like this you expect an older crowd, reliving their golden years, but the mass of the crowd skewed from their late twenties to early forties, waiting to hear somebody sing the mega swamp pop hits like "Sea of Love" or "When the Last Teardrops Fall" as if they were current pop hits. Every time, I have to overcome my jaded incredulousness: these people really like this music. Fifty-year-old songs have a currency with this community that contemporary pop artists would kill for. It is true love, without a shred of irony.

I generally shy away from festivals in this book, despite their being a huge part of the Louisiana musical landscape, only because they are special occasions. They are not the everyday, but I am including the Swamp Pop Festival because I got the feeling that its audience would come out every weekend for this kind of event.

My friend and I were stationed behind two older gals with T-shirts advertising the Cajun radio powerhouse KBON 101.1 FM from Eunice. The radio station's tagline is Louisiana

Proud, but its shirts boasted a more precise slogan: "Hey babe, where da ice chest at?" The women pushed toward the front when swamp pop legend Tommy McClain took the stage. In his heyday, McClain had the rugged charm of a young Waylon Jennings with a voice like a teenager from heaven. His biggest claim to fame was as the writer of Freddy Fender's "If You Don't Leave Me Alone (Leave Me Alone)" and for his own rendition of "Sweet Dreams," which sold three million copies in 1966. He played with country singer Clint West in the Boogie Kings, one of the great swamp pop supergroups in the 1960s.

McClain's pipes have seen better days; he can't hit those heartbreaking high notes like he once could, but that hasn't tarnished his star quality a bit. Bedecked in a glitter vest and white cowboy hat, McClain worked the crowd like Wayne Newton does a Vegas floorshow. I looked back, and under that massive mirror ball, older couples danced among twentysomethings bellowing along to the lyrics of every old regional hit as if it had just come out that week.

The guy I was there to see was the headliner, Warren Storm. Despite being the drummer who played on so many of the blues sides that came out of J. D. Miller's studio in Crowley in the fifties, besides being one of the founders of swamp pop when he and the late Bobby Charles would check out black New Orleans rhythm and blues clubs in the fifties and then work that into the pop music of the region, Warren Storm is my sartorial hero. Sporting white bucks and silk shirts that shimmer like stars reflected on a placid mountain lake, a helmet of jet black hair, and maybe the perfect mustache, Warren Storm is a guy I hope to one day be cool enough to emulate.

He's a peerless singer to boot, seemingly guiding an old schmaltzy relic like "Seven Letters" into the air like a wizard, all the while singing from behind a drum kit. It's like the fifties never ended, and I suppose that is the allure of swamp pop. The late fifties and early sixties were when Louisiana culture was starting to gain its pride back, when singers like Warren

Swamp Pop Music Festival

Storm and Tommy Mc-Clain could contend with the big names. That era is one that also, divorced from any political or historical reality, is considered a golden era by a lot of Americans. I don't know if any of this really plays into the minds of swamp pop fans, though more than anything, their love of these old tunes, their identification with them, are enough to keep that era going for at least another generation.

The Black Pearl

UPSCALE AFRICAN AMERICAN "GROWN FOLKS" CLUB; OPEN ON SPECIAL OCCASIONS

1854 Hwy. 190 W
Port Allen, LA
70767
(225) 773-3358

I'd seen a number of elaborate posters for shows at the Black Pearl around the neighborhood between downtown Baton Rouge and the Garden District, one of many spots on the racial patchwork of the city that most of my contemporaries never venture into. The posters were massive, printed on heavy card stock in old-fashioned block print, throwbacks to old playbills from the sixties. I scoured the Web for any references and found a single mention on an LSU sports–themed message board where someone asked why he saw a bunch of cars parked around what he'd assumed was an old abandoned club called the Black Pearl on Highway 190. Someone responded, bolstered by the Internet's scrim of anonymity, "I hear it gets pretty dark in there." I happened upon another of the club's posters, for an Easter show with R&B acts Vince Hutchinson and Jeff Floyd. I figured it was time.

I walked into an enormous hall lined with a bar on one side, mirrors on the other, and tables and chairs leading to a stage seemingly at the horizon. The folks already assembled in the hall were dressed to the nines—men in slick suits and hats, women in décolletage and shimmering finery. They were clothed like grown folks ready to party. It made me realize I dress like a teenager most of the time and that, sartorially, I was clearly out of my league at the Black Pearl. Just as I was thinking that the woman in the jaw-dropping gold lamé and fringe dress with matching boots was the most elaborately outfitted I was going to see this evening, Vince Hutchinson and the Heavy Storm Band took to the stage in African-style robes, looking like Earth, Wind & Fire in their prime.

The eight-member group operated with a precision that matched their outfits. The funk got rolling with "Love Don't Live Here No More," a classic R&B

groove demonstrating that heartbreak and joy are but two sides of the same emotional coin. Vince peppers his songs with dead-on stage banter, rendering them into conversations with the audience. It created an intimacy that I don't get from most of the concerts I attend. When his big number "Player Hater" came up, people were leaving their chairs and dancing in the aisles. I love the way soul music operates. Its smooth contours don't give you anything easy to latch onto, but then it seeps under your skin and brings you to your feet. By the time he got to his final number, a resplendent version of the late James Brown's "It's a Man's World," the room was moving in lockstep with the same cosmic groove the band was working.

I took the intermission as a chance to procure one of the catfish plates I saw people eating and talk with the proprietor, Darryll Brown, about his club. "I wanted to bring in acts so that folks around here wouldn't have to go too far to see a nice show," says Brown of the club he's run for three years. "It's big enough to accommodate a big act but lets them get a little close, to really feel it." Evidently, the rest of the club had the same idea I did, so Darryll went back to taking orders and I took my plate to the nearest empty table to devour my catfish. Fried catfish is maybe my favorite thing ever, so I was fully engrossed in the Black Pearl's excellent rendition of it as the main act, Jeff Floyd's band, was tuning up.

Jeff Floyd has a jazzier take on soul than the funk-fortified opening act, with a horn section, full band, and phalanx of backup singers in slinky dresses, all in black. Floyd came out in an orange outfit and sunglasses and launched directly into an incendiary love bomb of a song. Again, the lockstep of all those musicians working to stoke the fires of soul is going to make it hard to take the ramshackle groups I usually go out to see. Floyd croons and screams and wails like a man possessed. Suffice to say, I like what they got out there, or rather, what we have out here should some of us be willing to explore it.

DETOUR:

Searching for Emma's

I n south Louisiana, it has been my experience that as far as nightclubs catering to traditional music go, the black and white worlds are separate ones, acknowledged by each other but rarely ventured into. I've never experienced any racial confrontation directed at me (though as a white male, I am generally not the target of such tensions), nor have I seen any pointed antagonism between the black and white worlds, but I have experienced an ignorance one of the other.

For a long time, Clarence "Pieman" Williams was listed in the *Advocate,* the Baton Rouge daily paper, as playing every Saturday at a blues club in Port Allen called Emma's. Port Allen is a slip of a town, strung out along the river across from the Baton Rouge downtown skyline. I asked around, and no one I knew had ever been to Emma's; few had even heard of it. I thought I might become acquainted with another Teddy's Juke Joint, a smoldering ember of a once white hot blues trail.

Decades ago, Port Allen, along with the adjacent section of West Baton Rouge Parish, was the Wild West. I've heard plenty of tales from wild nights at river clubs at the base of the Highway 190 bridge. One particularly salacious story from 1949 involved a young tenor saxophonist named Ornette Coleman, who was playing with New Orleans bandleader Silas Green at a club in Port Allen. Allegedly, Coleman kept injecting bebop licks into the band's dance material, and it enraged the crowd so much that they beat Coleman up and threw his saxophone in the river. Coleman switched to alto sax, moved out to Los Angeles with Pee Wee Clayton's band, and, almost a decade later, released *Something Else!!!!,* an album that fearlessly mixed the blues and jazz idioms and was a steppingstone toward Coleman being one of the most innovative musical figures of the century.

Apocryphal as this tale might be, I hoped to find some remnant of that fire at Emma's, if but a trace element of the complex and ferocious nature of the blues. But first I had to find the club. The address took me to a large hip-hop club on Highway 1 with cars parked in the median for blocks. I asked a few people on the street about Emma's, and nobody had ever heard of it. My asking was treated with general suspicion; one young woman asked if I was a cop. I crossed over to a gas station to ask an older black man sitting outside, who said he'd show me where it was if I bought him a beer. The gas station attendant had never heard of the place, so I took my new friend up on his offer, expecting little from the transaction, and sure enough, he waved me back to where I had just come from. "It's right there, man. You can't miss it." I asked him if he'd been there recently, and his recollections grew instantly fuzzy. "Yeah! Well, no, last Christmas I think it was. I don't know if they got anything going on tonight. It's the real deal though," he assured me. "They used to get me to play in there every Friday. No, every Saturday."

I walked back past the hip-hop club, wondering if Emma's was somehow in one of the dodgy-looking apartments next to it, and decided I wasn't quite up to risking it. I stepped into a daiquiri place next door and asked the bartender if he knew where Emma's was. "Lemme ask the waitress. She grew up around here." She shook her head from across the room, and the guy gestured toward the north wall of the building. "Never heard of it. Must be over in the black part. I don't know what they got over there." It hit home that the *black part* basically started just on the other side of that wall.

Magnolia Café
GREAT RESTAURANT AND COZY SCREENED-IN PORCH WITH LIVE CAJUN AND ROOTS MUSIC

5687 Commerce St.
St. Francisville, LA
70775
(225) 635-6528
themagnoliacafe.net/

I have plenty of encounters with sweet little towns and think, "I could live here," but the impulse really couldn't be stronger than when I find myself at the Magnolia Café in St. Francisville, watching a Cajun or folk or bluegrass band saw away with congenial abandon on that screened-in porch. I think if I lived in one of St. Francisville's many adorable restored homes that I bought with the proceeds of my wildly successful music-venue book, I could pad down to the Birdman for coffee in the morning, do a little writing just to keep my head in the game, hold court with the regulars, and then pop into the Mag for lunch and maybe again for dinner and whoever is gracing the cicadas and the clinking tableware with song.

Another St. Francisville fantasy involves much the same itinerary, except that I am a mysterious drifter of modest means who has holed up in one of the restored detached rooms of the vintage motor court lodge that rings the gravel parking lot. When the locals whisper to another, "What's his story?" the query is eventually dropped and I am allowed to be one of the many colorful characters who give this place its charm.

I lived in the Pacific Northwest in one of my few brief forays away from Louisiana, and one of the places I liked to frequent was called Third Place Books, a combination food court, bookstore, and coffee shop. I liked it not so much for the amenities of the place itself, but for the notion in its name—it's important to have a third place, something apart from home and work. It's a place that exists outside of your sphere of responsibility yet has all the familiarity of home. Having a favorite place is like having a favorite song. It moves you in a strange, familiar way, an intimate way. Like music, you experience it physically,

mechanically, without the need for analysis or understanding past the actual raw experience to get its value. It just happens, and that resonance stays with you.

St. Francisville is like a favorite album. It has all the necessary components: the mighty Mississippi River as its general flow, the eternal subdued heartbeat of Highway 61 maintaining its pace, and an organic array of quaint neighborhoods, moss-covered churches, timeless storefronts, and bustling restaurants as the different interlocking melodies. And on Commerce Street, right past Ferdinand, lies my favorite song on the album, an epic two-part track made of the Magnolia Café and Birdman Coffee and Books.

Until fame and fortune find me, I feel privileged to just visit St. Francisville. When I pulled up in the old motor court, flanked to the left by picturesque rental cabins and anchored by the Magnolia in the center, I saw the glowing neon "Open" sign protesting against the black still of the night. I was hypnotized by the smell of the food and the mixed clamor of laughter, silverware clicking on plates, and the infinite rhythms of Joe Hall (of Stomp Down Zydeco fame) and his Cajun trio. The Magnolia is one of those places that immediately feels like home. The restaurant occupies a small house that sits behind the original location, which burned to the ground in 2003, with walls festooned with vibrant local artwork and couples quietly huddled around whatever unbelievable special owner Robin Marshall has cooked up.

But, like any Cajun house worth its andouille, the real action takes place on the porch, and the Magnolia has the greatest screened-in porch of all time. It snakes around pockets of tables where people come from miles around to cackle and gossip and, perhaps, if the spirits in the room and from the adjacent full-service bar do their magic, take to the small dance floor in front of the stage.

Joe Hall's trio plugged away like only a Cajun group can, the accordion and fiddle trading on undulating variations of

Exterior of Magnolia Café (Photo by Peter Verbois, psverbois .zenfolio.com)

ancient waltzes and shuffles. Layer in the aroma of the food and the cheer of the customers wafting through the perfect breeze on the porch, and it is hard to imagine a more perfect choice to claim as one's home.

CAJUN COUNTRY

Richard Sale Barn

UNIQUE PERFORMANCE VENUE MADE FROM AN OLD CATTLE AUCTION BARN; BLUES, CAJUN, AND ZYDECO MUSIC ON THE THIRD SATURDAY OF EVERY MONTH (CLOSED DURING THE SUMMER)

1307 South Henry St.
Abbeville, LA
70510
lebayou.org

On Abbeville's Henry Street, I pulled into the parking lot of a seafood place named Richard's and asked my travel companions, "Is this it?" Andrea, an Abbeville native, shook her head "no" and called her dad, who explained that the Richard Sale Barn, our curious destination for this trip, was "down Power Pump Road before you get to Richard's." This is the kind of directions to which I've become accustomed on trips like this: Richard's is before Richard's, and Power Pump Road is what the locals call Henry Street. The obscurity involved in getting to a place has generally proven to be a harbinger of its beauty. We turned around and spied a tiny yellow sign at a break in the trees and joined the cars shimmied into the makeshift parking lot.

This little spot on the Vermilion River has been a gathering place since the 1940s, when Jean Richard Avery started showing off and selling cattle arriving by barge under shade trees on the lot. Richard's reputation as a square dealer brought more people in, and in 1946 he erected the auction barn under the name Abbeville Commission Company. The building was set up with a semicircular chute, allowing the cattle to be paraded before a terraced amphitheater of farmers and businessmen shouting bids to the auctioneer on a small stage. Once a final price was reached, the animal was led into a weighing room under the platform. It was an efficient setup and likely quite a show, with the auctioneer vacillating between English and French, money changing hands.

The Tuesday afternoon auctions were a fixture on the Abbeville social calendar up through the seventies when the business closed. Over the years the building has seen use as a saddle shop—the owner Jean Avery Richard III still trains horses in back—but on

Abbeville

the evening I went, and every third Saturday, the crowd was assembled for a very different kind of spectacle. The building has
been converted to one of the most curious live-music venues
around.

The band on this occasion, Henry Gray & the Cats, sets
up on the auctioneers' stage, now gussied up with a tangle of
white Christmas lights and a curtain stenciled with horses and
palmetto leaves. In fact, the whole place is festooned to the
rafters. Old, rusted local signage and farm tools are tacked up
everywhere. A display case of spurs occupies the lobby, where
a makeshift bar has been set up. As I climbed the terraced
wooden seating to get to the top, I spied a dried cow skull sitting
next to a Fellini poster, which is the best talisman I've ever seen.

The room was near capacity. Andrea saw a couple of rela-
tives in the mix. Former Howlin' Wolf pianist and blues legend
Henry Gray is a treasure, culturally speaking, but you got the
feeling that come show night, the whole of Abbeville headed
out to the Barn. In fact, as the emcee explained the upcoming
schedule, she apologized for having this show on the second
Saturday in March; there was an event scheduled somewhere
else in town on the third one. Evidently there is not enough
Abbeville to go around for two events at once.

The seating is flat and hard going for a whole show, so regulars bring stadium chairs or, more popular, sofa cushions, which
only adds to the place's homey charm. Before the house lights
dim, I ask my crew if they want another beer, and a woman
next to us chimes in that she wants one. I bring one for her in
the name of small-town neighborliness.

The sight lines might be a little limited on the bottom
rows facing the metal gate around the old weighing room
now crammed full with saddles, but otherwise this place is a
remarkably good live-music venue. The announcer said they
take June through August off because it's simply too hot in the
building, but it is perfect on this cool March evening. The lights
dim, except for those Christmas lights circling the stage, and
Gray kicks it into gear.

Henry Gray and the Cats
at the Richard Sale Barn

The band is in strong form despite losing their longtime harmonica player, Brian "B. B." Bruce, to cancer. A few heartfelt words are said about the celebrated harmonica player by bassist and band manager Andy Corbett, who picked up the harmonica duties for the evening, but this was less a night for mourning than it was for rock and blues at its most primal. Gray was born in Kenner but grew up on a farm in Alsen, just north of Baton Rouge, where he honed his piano skills and eventually became the piano player for Howlin' Wolf. His résumé is a primer of the blues: Jimmy Reed, Skip James, Muddy Waters, Elmore James—you'd be hard pressed to name a famous blues musician Henry Gray hasn't played with.

That provenance is demonstrated throughout the evening with Wolf's "Little Red Rooster" and Muddy's "Rock Me." Gray pounds out his "two-fisted boogie-woogie" sitting at his keyboard solid as a fallen meteor center stage, counterbalanced by the impish charm of his drummer, the impeccably natty Earl "The Bishop" Christopher. Marti Christian is a hell of a guitarist, sending these timeworn blues stomps occasionally into the stratosphere, but the Cats move as a pack, eventually inspiring dancing on the vertiginous top rows and down in the cattle chute. By the close of the show, nearly two hours with a break for beer and autographs, the bar is a massive stomping whole. It's a wonder that cow skulls and Fellini posters and the whole history of Abbeville nightlife didn't come raining down on us, but I guess classics like Henry Gray and Jean Avery's barn are built to last.

Nunu's

COMBINATION DANCE HALL AND MEETING PLACE ACTIVELY ENGAGED IN BOTH THE FUTURE
AND PAST OF ACADIANA CULTURE

1510 Hwy. 93
(Old Singleton Lumber
Building)
Arnaudville, LA
70512
(337) 453-3307
frederickarts.home-
stead.com/

When we talk of attractions, we like to think that they are naturally occurring phenomena waiting there for us to discover. That's the perverse, egotistic joy of exploration: to think some roadside restaurant or perfect riverbank or stretch of scenic highway has been just sitting there, muddling along waiting for us to happen by and complete the circuit. It's a fallacy, of course, but one that works in everyone's favor.

The truth is that most destinations come about as a mix of happenstance and determination. Someone has a place, an idea, and then the river flow of the Universe turns it into what it will eventually become or washes it away. We, the travelers, are part of that river, with each paddle stroke, each time we pull over to shore; we help direct its course.

There is something to find at every destination—good or bad or both. On my way to Arnaudville to check out the scene artist George Marks has set up, I stopped at the Tiger Truck Stop in Grosse Tete to witness the "live tiger exhibit" I've seen advertised from the highway for years but have always been too afraid to stop at. The truck stop is just that, a fuel-up station with a staggering assortment of beef jerky available at the counter, which would make it a favorite in my book were it not for the tiger pacing in the cage exposed to the elements, out between the trailer of trucker showers and the frontage road. It's a painful tableau to witness, and while I have no doubt that the tiger is adequately tended to and cared for, this is the kind of attraction I can do without.

George Marks's complex in Arnaudville is more what I was after. It started when the artist moved back to his hometown as a pit stop on his way to New York and never left. He opened his gallery/studio in a building right on Highway 31, just before the bridge

Arnaudville

across Bayou Fuselier, titling it Town Market Centre. He opened a kitchen in the back (serving beer, wine, and delicious pressed sandwiches) and started booking Cajun and roots bands in the cavernous main room, and Nunu's was born.

The place has a smart, theatrical, yet homespun design that sets it apart from any Cajun dance club I've been to. Artwork from Marks and other artists adorns the walls, and the dance floor, with its track light perimeter and black background, is weirdly glamorous. "Preserve, promote, and perpetuate, without becoming a theme park," Marks says of his club. "We want to be true to the area without being contrived."

The locals seem to buy in. Nunu's holds a Table de Français on the last Saturday of every month for French-speakers of all ages to meet and gossip. "We had seventy-three people signed in," says Mavis Frugé. "L. J. Melancon brought in his accordion and Louie Michot brought his fiddle and we had an impromptu performance." This kind of spirit permeates the way Marks runs the business. "We had one group come in that asked if they could have a mandolin player join in on their Cajun group. I said, 'Sure, why not?' and it was a hit with the audience."

The truest test of community acceptance was passed that evening when the Lost Bayou Ramblers kicked in with their first waltz, and the dance floor immediately filled up. I saw a number of familiar faces from other Cajun dance clubs in the area, mixed with a lot of younger people, some barefoot, some in cowboy boots, but all moving in that beautiful way the accordion commands of its listeners. The Lost Bayou Ramblers mirror Nunu's in a lot of ways. They are definitely steeped in the traditions of where they are from, but they have a more playful, relaxed approach to it. Cajun bands often seem like they are trying to out-tradition each other, catering to the hotshots on the dance floor, but the Ramblers' rhythms hover more toward midtempo and were frankly more inviting than I'm used to. At one point, a line dance broke out, with some joining in and with others orbiting in two-step formation. It was a beautiful sight.

Marks says that Nunu's and Town Market Centre are set up

for possibilities. "We are talking about building a big screened-in porch out back, and possibly having some floating kitchens out on the bayou," he says. "One of our regular performers has mentioned wanting to barbecue out back, and I can picture him entering the dance floor, discarding his apron and chef's hat, and taking his place on the stage. We are always trying to encourage people to do something they wouldn't normally do."

In 2009, Town Market Centre suffered a number of tragedies: a car crashed into the side of the building, and then a fire tore through it as soon as it reopened. True to Marks's determined spirit, they have set up shop in the old Singleton Lumber Building and are in the process of rebuilding Nunu's to its former glory.

Tom's Fiddle and Bow

INSTRUMENT REPAIR SHOP WITH COZY PERFORMANCE SPACE IN THE FRONT; CAJUN MUSIC JAM ON SUNDAY AFTERNOONS

204 Fuselier St.
Arnaudville, LA
70512
(337) 754-5528
tomsfiddleandbow.com

Tom Pierce couldn't have possibly mapped out his road to Arnaudville in advance. "I was working in the shipyard in Portsmouth, Maine," he told me as he took a break from the informal Sunday jam session taking place in the front room of his shop. "I got into Cajun and bluegrass music in the mid nineties and I met Lori [his future bride] at a dance in 1999 in Long Island. Our first date didn't work out, and we went our separate ways for three years." The two met up again at a coffee shop in 2002, and this time the relationship clicked. "Soon as we met, she told me, 'I'm moving to Louisiana,' and I told her if you wait until I retire, I'll go with you. In 2005 I retired, we got married, and we moved, just like that." On a trip to Louisiana to look for houses, the couple stumbled upon Arnaudville. "Driving around, we got lost here. I looked around and saw a quiet sleepy little town and thought, 'This is a nice place.'"

On Sunday afternoons, the nicest thing happens at this nice place. Tom hosts what he dubs the "organic jam"—a jam session where things are a little more free-form than your typical Cajun jam, letting country, folk, and rock seep into the edges. "Some days we have a bluegrass band up front and a French band going out here," referring to the breezy porch overlooking the bayou. That afternoon, a gaggle of fiddlers and accordionists assembled in the front parlor and started working through some tunes. The room was at capacity, so I took that as an opportunity to tour the workshop.

The walls were lined with racks filled with violin bodies in various states of repair. Tom's work tables were covered with chisels, clamps, boxes of parts. He showed the violin he had made from scratch, a pris-

Organic jam at Tom's
Fiddle and Bow

tine assembly of bent spruce and maple ringed with meticulous hand-carved inlays. "When I started doing this, I thought that carving the curls on the head would be the hard part, and it takes some time, but the real difficult part is carving the f-holes," Tom explained. The f-holes are the ornately curved holes in the top of the instrument that allow the sound to escape from the resonating chamber. "I think it's because you've labored for so long getting this thing just right, bending the wood and getting the panels precise like that, and now you have to punch a hole in it!"

Tom went on to explain some of the further geometric intricacies of the instrument, things like the three-degree angle in the joint between the neck and the body of the instrument that created the tension necessary for the instrument to function. Looking at so many violins in varying states of completeness, I remarked that it was all tension and balance; everything had to be shaped exactly so and connected in the right place for it to work. "It's amazing how much pressure you have on that bridge," he said, pointing to the small wedge of wood that hoists the high-tension strings at the precise angle over the fret board. "There is something like 140 foot-pounds of pressure at this one point!"

Just then laughter erupted from the parlor. They eased into another song, but one of the fiddlers started laughing again and lost count and the whole thing had to start over. Everyone seemed cool with this loose organization, in contrast to the careful precision with which a lot of Cajun musicians ply their art. I'm thankful that there are so many musicians who hold fast and true to the tradition; they are the reason the culture still exists, but I'm equally glad there is a corner of Acadiana where the pressure is off.

D.I.'s Cajun Restaurant

FAMILY-STYLE CAJUN RESTAURANT WITH LARGE DANCE FLOOR AND LIVE CAJUN MUSIC THURSDAY, FRIDAY, AND SATURDAY NIGHTS

6561 Evangeline Hwy.
Basile, LA
70515
(337) 432-5141
discajunrestaurant.biz

The whole south of Louisiana on Interstate 10 is the epitome of flatness, but in the clouds as I rolled through Jennings, the sunset was a pink mountain against a smeared gold sky. When I turned up the Evangeline Highway toward Basile, those pink mountains were whittled down by the oncoming night. As I pulled into D.I.'s, a Cajun family restaurant plotted in a rectangle carved out of the rice fields, those imaginary peaks had dissipated into a deep, lulling azure. I highly recommend you work a sunset into your itinerary when traveling this part of the state.

The restaurant operates with that high-meets-low Cajun sense of upscale—$20 entrees with homey appeal accompanied by a wicker basket of crackers. The blond-paneled walls were adorned with a framed portrait of the Iota High football team from when they made it to the finals in 2004, stuffed and mounted ducks, and a framed accolade about their food from *Gourmet* magazine.

What I like about a place like D.I.'s is that it is a relaxed combination of social and private. Long tables of families are each helmed by a convivial loudmouth with a Bud Light—one is declaring LSU didn't really deserve its win earlier in the day against Ole Miss, another is disparaging the quality of someone's BBQ beans recipe at the tailgate, but it's an easy interaction. Guards are down.

Briggs Brown and the Bayou Cajuns play the waltzes and two-steps with more than the casual nod to Hank Williams and the classic country of the fifties and sixties that nearly wiped Cajun music out of existence, but is still perfectly danceable music, perhaps even more so than strict Cajun music. Gaggles of squirrelly girls pair up and two-step around the

Basile

large wooden dance floor, while a few other kids scurry around moms next to me, each focused on platters of boiled crabs. Briggs Brown and band have already sung their second happy birthday of the evening by the time my perfunctory salad arrived. I think about ordering the crabs, but my appetite after the drive outweighs my skill at extracting the meat.

Gourmet wasn't kidding; the food is good at D.I.'s. Its "Catfish Billy"—lightly battered and fried filets topped with tangy crawfish étouffée—can hold its own with much fancier joints. But I wasn't here for the food; I was here for the band and to see how couples make their way around the dance floor on the western edge of Acadiana. The weird thing, though, is no one was dancing but the kids.

A third happy birthday! The band has settled into a swing, and a few adults, having adequately digested their platters of crab, finally venture out for a spin, but this is no Breaux Bridge.

My waitress explained that they had a tradition of kids' dancing in these parts originating in the Wednesday night "family dances" at the Four Corners Inn down in Crowley, the one night a week when the rough-and-tumble roadhouse behaved itself and let the kids hang out with the adults. When I remarked on the contrast between this scene and that of Cajun dance floors just twenty miles to the east, she plainly stated, "Well, what we do is more of a traditional Cajun than down in Breaux Bridge."

I was dumbfounded. I couldn't imagine anyone attempting to out-Cajun the most Cajun place in the world, but halfway through my catfish entrée, I came around to her point. This was the authentic Cajun, westernized—even if it was only twenty miles west—by the massive popularity of country music, homogenized into the greater culture of America. We were about as close to Beaumont as we were to Breaux Bridge; it made sense that culturally we were in between the two.

Café Des Amis

MID-PRICED, ADORABLE CAJUN RESTAURANT WITH ZYDECO BANDS SATURDAY MORNINGS AND SOME EVENINGS

140 East Bridge St.
Breaux Bridge, LA
70517
(337) 332-5273
cafedesamis.com/

I am picturing a retirement-age couple in an RV, traipsing across America as they'd always planned, thumbing through guidebooks of the American South for ways to experience this "Cajun" culture they've heard so much about. They see the phrase "zydeco brunch" and a friendly name like Café Des Amis and think this sounds like a perfect morning stop before heading out west to see the new grandbaby in Houston. Little would they suspect that they would be pulling into the eye of a joyous storm.

Café Des Amis rests at one end of the slip of old downtown Breaux Bridge, or "Pont Breaux," as the locals often refer to it, among quaint antique shops and the errant business that bely the maelstrom inside. Our traveling couple might suspect something is amiss when they are asked to pay a cover and get a paper bracelet like one finds at a nightclub, given that it is 9 a.m. on a Saturday. Once through the door, they are confronted with full-force zydeco, a near deafening roar of accordion and hyperkinetic rhythm, and the tables where breakfast is being served lie on the other end of this swarm.

Even though I know what I'm getting into, I tend to get shaken awake when arriving at Café Des Amis's door. Recently, I found myself standing on the periphery, jotting down a few notes as my buddy Clarke fetched us a pair of Bloody Marys, the best fortification for this kind of mayhem, when a woman swung through the crowd like she was traversing a jungle canopy by vine and tapped my little notebook. "We don't want any of that wonky music critic bullshit in here. This place is for the dancers." I was a little thrilled

Breaux Bridge

to be recognized as the kind of blowhard that needs to be called out, and though I might debate my relative wonkiness, I will concede that she was absolutely right on the second part; the dancers own the room.

The building dates from the 1890s, when it was a general store, and has served as a casket factory, a dress shop, and, in 1992, a coffee shop cum art studio when Dickie Breaux, a former Louisiana state representative, bought the place. He started serving catfish, but over time the menu grew into one of the most celebrated in the region. My Bloody Mary arrived from the ornate bar salvaged from the old Evangeline Hotel in Lafayette. In 1998, Mr. Breaux added the zydeco brunch to his repertoire.

We made our way to the logjam of tables in the back. The rest of the week, Café Des Amis is a regular restaurant with normally spaced seating, but on Saturday mornings, the dancers demanded floor space. We were seated with a young couple from Alexandria, in the central part of the state, forced to shout our introductions over the band.

I fear I am painting Café Des Amis in a bad light, but trust me, eat the pickled okra from your second Bloody Mary and you will be well acclimated to the proceedings. I ordered the House Rock 'n' Special, starring andouille grits and a fried boudin patty and a side of *couche couche,* a traditional Cajun cornmeal mush served warm with cane syrup, and remembered to show my wristband to get my $5 admission price off the meal. All was right in the universe, and this proved a perfect vantage point for the dance floor.

Corey "Lil' Pop" Ledet and his band were crammed into a bay window in the front of the store while the dancers occupied all available space the way gas molecules do a container's volume, seemingly ricocheting off each other yet interlocking in their orbits. Ledet is a mercurial player, able to adapt his music to any situation, and that morning he proffered a style that skews closer to the Cajun side of the zydeco equation, leaning heavier on the accordion than the racing pulse of the rhythm section. He gave in to Cajun music's swing, its galloping simple rhythm, while holding on to the syncopated frenzied undercurrent that gives zydeco its power. It's the right mix for this situation, cutting the formality of Cajun waltzes and two-steps with a little wildness. Every minute or so, Ledet would let out a booming "YAH!" making our new friends from Alexandria jump each time.

"We've never seen anything like this!" our dining companions shouted over their breakfast after taking up my offer of a bite of *couche couche*. Alexandria is only an hour and a half up I-49 from nearby Lafayette but in many ways is a whole different world. When I asked about zydeco and Cajun music clubs out that way, they mentioned a dance at the Moose Lodge every month but again, gesturing to the room, "nothing like this."

Like Ledet's music, Café Des Amis is a perfect mix of the traditional holdover and the aggressive expansion of the culture. Mr. Breaux is responsible for much of the preservation of old Pont Breaux, and with Café Des Amis as its fiery locus, Cajun culture is safe in his hands.

The zydeco brunch lasts until 11:30 a.m., but shortly before it reached its crescendo, we bid our new friends adieu and ambled around the corner to Fly's for a cappuccino and its weekly Cajun music jam.

Fly's Coffee House (formerly The Coffee Break)
COFFEE SHOP WITH TRADITIONAL CAJUN MUSIC ON SATURDAY AFTERNOONS

109 North Main St.
Breaux Bridge, LA
70517
(337) 442-6607
facebook.com/
FlysCoffeeHouse

The older folks chatting at tables and the circle of folding chairs around the stage area implied a less frenetic take on Cajun music, but as it happens, it's a good thing I got some coffee, for there is not a gentle side to the Cajun accordion. A small group of French-speaking older musicians assembled and with little ado launched into a set of old-style Cajun music, waltzes and two-steps metered out with seasoned steadiness.

It is a very different thing to experience Cajun music off the dance floor; it removes its utilitarian aspect, to serve the dancers, and allows its simplistic charms to shine. At this particular jam session that takes place in quiet solemnity just a block away from the raging storm up the street (at Café Des Amis), it becomes folk music once again, the laments and exhortations of a struggling people, the idle moments, the fiery romances, the history of the Cajun exile from Canada to Louisiana all contained in a handful of chords and a simple take on waltz time.

The back room of Fly's is dotted with posters advertising French film festivals that feature music from the region and flyers for events in nearby Lafayette. I gravitate toward any and all CD racks in places like this and am drawn to one in particular: Gérard Dôle's *The Devil's Daughter,* its cover by famed underground comics icon R. Crumb featuring a wild-haired crone. Dôle came to America an ardent Hank Williams nut; his love for the song "Jambalaya" brought him to Louisiana and convinced Dôle to become a Cajun musician and to return to France to bring this music back to its linguistic point of origin. Dôle's albums are feral takes on traditional Cajun, invoking wild times on the mosquito-filled bayous, young men and women dancing barefoot in the grass. Perhaps Dôle's imagined version is closer to the long-lost Cajun tradition

Breaux Bridge

of house parties than is the reverent circle of musicians in the coffee shop. Maybe it's somewhere in between. I wonder how Dôle's CDs even ended up here, but then these are the kinds of questions that truly form a culture, an ebb and flow among feedback lines of which no one is in particular control.

La Poussiere

CLASSIC CAJUN DANCE HALL WITH CAJUN BANDS ON FRIDAY AND SATURDAY NIGHTS

1301 Grand Pointe Ave.
Breaux Bridge, LA
70517
(337) 332-1721
lapoussiere.com

One of the first trips I made with my buddy Clarke was to introduce a bunch of Louisiana newcomers to how it's done at La Poussiere in Breaux Bridge. La Poussiere has occupied the same unassuming low-slung building since moving from across the street in 1976. The parking lot was as packed as the hall, but somehow we managed to score one of the few remaining tables set around the immense dance floor, and after a bucket of Miller High Life and witnessing the Pine Leaf Boys starting their set, we were ready for immersion.

La Poussiere (French for "the dust," after the sawdust that would get sprinkled on the dance floor) is a purely functional yet congenial establishment. The bulk of the room is taken up with a dance floor—where old Cajun couples two-step and waltz in gorgeous precision—with a stage at one end and a bar at the other. We all took a shot at the floor at one point, politely trying not to run everyone off the tracks. Cajun dance is a peculiar mix of intimacy and ceremony. The idea that these couples go out nearly every Saturday night to dance, for years, as long as they can still make it around the floor, is one of the most beautiful things about Cajun culture. The dancing is a thread woven into the seamless texture of everyday life in this part of the country. Sure, there are some couples that are the obvious hotshots, like the gentleman with a headband who flung his partner around the room with a fencer's dexterity, but what touched me were the couples who moved in slow processions counterclockwise, their steps not much more than synchronized walking. One's acumen is not the important part; it's the participation that counts. This sense of purpose, propriety even, is largely what keeps the Cajuns a living, breathing culture.

I took a few spins with my friends

around the dance floor, but the Krewe de Canaille dance club was in the house that evening, and they were not going to let my clumsiness disrupt the symbiosis between the room and the band. The Pine Leaf Boys are a devastatingly good band, taking the lost songs their grandparents played and bringing them back to life with equal parts reverence and revelry. I watched from the side with a piece of cake (note to future places I visit: have cake, which makes everything better) as my friends were routinely swept up into the fray. Part of what intrigues me about Cajun music is how it forms a continuum that seems to just shift the beats and tempo around, and the night goes on and on with the sound powering the room.

Come 11 p.m., we were exhausted, unlike the folks twice our age who were still going strong, so we bid our adieus and headed home. I'm always floored by the aggressive cling Pont Breaux has on its heritage. It goes beyond restoring the buildings downtown or maintaining the French language. It's a deeper thing than pride. It's an understanding that there is nothing else like this and it's worth keeping.

Mulate's

THE ORIGINAL CAJUN RESTAURANT WITH CAJUN MUSIC EVERY EVENING

325 West Mills Ave.
Breaux Bridge, LA
70517
(337) 332-4648
mulates.com/
breauxbridge.html

Some traditions in Breaux Bridge seem to be barely hanging on. Take Mulate's, the venerable restaurant and dance hall out on the back road to Lafayette. Mulate's is considered by many to be the original Cajun restaurant and for years was the default place to send out-of-town visitors to get a dose of Cajun culture.

Outside, two large paintings of dancers stand on either side of the aging facade, as if the logical union between the man and woman in a community setting, the dance, can be found right about where their gazes meet on the dance floor. They are my two favorite pieces of Cajun folk art, and if I were the tattooing sort, I might sport copies of them on my shoulder blades.

In the early 1950s Mulate Guidry bought the old Rendez-vous Club in Henderson, one of many dance halls that dotted the roads through the swamp, and moved it to Breaux Bridge, renaming it for himself. Over the years, Mulate's has stood as a bastion of Cajun food and music. I was on my way back from Lafayette one night after searching for a club called Shangri-La—this is not a metaphor; my neighbors said they went to such a place somewhere out that way once—and the longing in those two dancers on the murals reminded me it had been a month or two since I had had some gumbo and maybe a decade since I'd been to Mulate's. The building was closed for a long time after a fire, but once I passed the proud plaque of luminaries, both local musicians and visiting big names, I spied the swamp mural around the place and the carved alligator at the edge of the dance floor, and I realized the place hadn't changed a bit.

Besides a family holding a birthday party across a number of pushed-together tables, I was the only other customer that night. The band still played on, a group of young men who

Breaux Bridge

had chosen to take up the accordion and the washboard and t-fer (triangle) in defiance of the passing of Mulate's heyday.

The grandma across the way—I suspect also the birthday girl—called out for "Jolie Blonde," the "Brown-Eyed Girl" of Cajun tunes—not a bad song by any stretch, but it's the one they always ask for. The band launched amiably into the song's minor key lope, and one of the younger men in the party took Grandma out on the dance floor. Just then my gumbo arrived as well.

It was not the best "Jolie Blonde" performance I've ever heard, nor was it the best gumbo, but I loved it all the more because it was still here. Cajun culture is not fancy; in fact, its humility verges at times on aggressive restraint, on a need to titrate anything extra out of the mix. I imagined this scene to be the usual reality of the Cajun house parties of long ago, where a family band would go by boat from house to house along the bayou and play on Saturday nights. It didn't matter that they weren't the best band in the area, playing to the best dancers in the best places; this little gathering was content to simply still exist in this fashion, and I felt it a privilege to look on. Only time will tell how long that privilege will be available.

Club LA

NO-FRILLS BACKWOODS ZYDECO CLUB; ZYDECO BANDS ON SATURDAY NIGHTS AND AFTER TRAIL RIDES

2043 Coteau Rodaire Hwy.
Cecilia, LA
70512

It was one of those nights that looked like it wasn't going to pan out; my frequent running partner Clarke and I had been out at the Blue Moon Saloon in Lafayette to see Chubby Carrier and the Bayou Swamp Band fete their latest CD, *Zydeco Junkie*. I can't really fault Chubby Carrier; he's an affable performer who gives the curiosity of zydeco a congenial, smiling makeover, but it just wasn't taking. A friend of mine calls what they play "zydeco for America," and he's on point; *Zydeco Junkie* won the zydeco/Cajun Grammy in 2011. America may not be so keen on the relationship, though, for the zydeco/Cajun award was rolled into a broader "roots" category.

We stopped at Taco Bell at one of the Lafayette exits in acquiescence to this greater America on our way home when I thought to dial up the Patsy Report on my phone. The Patsy Report is an online guide of Cajun and zydeco events throughout the country maintained by Arn Burkoff, a Louisiana music nut based out of New Jersey. It had a listing for J. Paul Jr. and the Zydeco NuBreeds playing an after-party for a zydeco trail ride at the Club LA just off the next exit in Cecilia. We left our Taco Supremes on the table.

To get to Club LA, you take the Highway 347 exit, northbound, off I-10 and you drive. And you drive and drive. This part started to seem familiar, like the first night I went out to Teddy's Juke Joint in Zachary, the first of many trips on this journey. The loneliness of a country road has often proven to be a good sign when seeking out the unexpected, and just as soon as we were certain we missed it, there in the flattened muck of a rice field were parked a smattering of pickups and a building that looked like it had been dropped from the sky as if to squash a witch. "This must be the place," I thought.

Once we were subjected to a metal detector sweep and

Cecilia

paid out ten dollars, we found ourselves in the midst of cowboys mingling in the dark. Zydeco clubs have a tendency to be inadequately lit, but there were exactly two lights on in the whole of the club, one bare bulb servicing both the bar and the pool table in the back, and a workman's clip lamp over a makeshift shots bar set up to one side of the dance floor. Trail riders bedecked in cowboy hats and matching vests for their particular trail ride crew cut sharp shadows into the glare from the shots bar.

After acclimating to the dark and downing a beer or two, I started to get a sense of the room. The building had likely been a small church at one point. The dance floor occupied a long room with a pitched roof that terminated in a low stage where J. Paul Jr. was setting up, impossibly, without lights. I noticed that at even two-yard intervals metal cables were strung taut across the ceiling. I pointed these out to Clarke, who, ever the architect, had already taken notice. He said they were most likely holding the place together.

J. Paul Jr. and the Zydeco NuBreeds slid into their set like a snake entering a swamp. His nickname being "The Rebel," J. Paul Jr. bucks the usual hyperkinetic beat and pounding rhythms of zydeco for R&B, mixing his melodic accordion lines with that of a keyboard. It is full-on slow-jam zydeco. It was remarkable to me that after five years of scouring the landscape for a holistic picture of Louisiana music, another wrinkle should appear. J. Paul Jr.'s music was happy, lyrical, forlorn, imbued with the past and seeking the future all at once. I thought of the millions of bad party bands I've endured and wished that this was the music used instead. Then when the last song slid into a close, the room seemed to barely take notice. Not that the patrons weren't enjoying the band; you could make out the odd couple dancing out there at the edge of darkness. It was instead the interweaving of the music and this group of people: silken R&B booty jams for black, French-speaking cowboys in the pitch-dark bar in the middle of a rice field. It felt like highly specialized evolution.

Pat Davis Club

LARGE ZYDECO DANCE HALL IN A CONVERTED BARN; LIVE ZYDECO MUSIC ON SPORADIC SATURDAY NIGHTS AND AFTER TRAIL RIDES

2655 Main Hwy.
Cecilia, LA
70521
(337) 667-4422

The Pat Davis Club in Cecilia is an embodiment of that evolution through which zydeco constantly goes; the trip to the club involves a considerable amount of doubling back through the small town of Cecilia along Main Highway, running parallel to the interstate but feeling miles away in the Acadiana countryside. The club resides in a converted barn, and were it not for the cars scattered around the gravel lot, my friend Clarke and I would have most likely missed it altogether. We parked out back, and as we made it up a rough plank walkway running alongside, I could hear Keith Frank's massive rhythm section shake the rafters. I wondered how rustic this was going to be.

Inside, the barn is completely refinished into a long, cavernous dance hall. On one side of the room is a long stretch of tables sparsely dotted with couples set under a low roof where stalls most likely once stood. Part of the area on the other side is filled in with a kitchen where a few women sell sausage and jambalaya, bobbing their heads, leaning out of the sliding window where the orders are taken as a circle of men bounce the end of their pool cues on the concrete floor, adding to the echoed percussive maelstrom that is Frank's band. A photographer was setting up a souvenir photo stand near the stacks of amps fitted with neon green "KF" logos. Otherwise, the place was empty at 10 p.m.

One of the main reasons why I love Keith Frank is that he is undeterred by such conditions. He and the Soileau Family Band in their two-drummer configuration were pounding out an almost stream-of-consciousness flow of zydeco's influences. One tune started out with a command to "Do the Zydeco Funk" and the lights were shut off, leaving only the green neon monograms to cast an unearthly glow on the room; the shadow of

Cecilia

Keith Frank at the Pat
Davis Club

the sole dancing couple reached almost to the pool tables.

Another song featuring a highly syncopated wood-block part throughout started with a hard-rock tangent, like they might lean into "Kashmir" any second but at the last moment veered off into Funkadelic's "swing down sweet chariot, let me ride" chant, then into a James Gang–style boogie breakdown around the phrase "It's alright." What's next, "Bohemian Rhapsody"? I felt like anything could be incorporated into it. Then a surf riff emerged, turning into a rock-steady reggae jam evolving into Frank's tune "Soul Survivor," revealing his reggae predilections. Frank's appropriation of Jamaican rhythms is akin to that found in dub, the hazy deconstructed cousin of reggae in which the songs are reduced to the baseline and the beats with the lyrics weaving in and out of the song, fragments. Frank can pull apart and then reassemble a song into something else on the fly, lacing it with a melancholy sweetness that reminds me of reggae's complex vibe. A sweet guitar lick escapes from the rumble of sound like bees escaping from the gables of a barn. The washboard player launches into a barker's rant not dissimilar to the hype man for a rapper, all while the twin drummers and bassist keep each other in a deafening geosynchronous orbit.

During a break, when the lights came back on, I inspected the stage area. It was set up with a barn motif, curiously contrasting the graffiti-esque murals that graced the walls around it. It was a barn within a barn that had been fixed up to not look like a barn. Arching over the rural backdrop were the words "Kountry Bunnies," the name of the trail-riding group that called the Davis Club its home base. This was a night that, for me, further opened up the idea of what zydeco is, or rather, revealed it to be a musical form unlike jazz, one that can draw on everything around it and contextualize it through that particular beat. It was an hour into the show and I wondered if anyone else was going to show up. I've been to other zydeco shows out in the country that were similarly sparsely attended. Is it the distance to the small communities where these clubs stand? Am I following the wrong zydeco performer? I asked the bartender when the crowd typically gets there, and he responded that they show up when they show up, if they show up.

The Hot Spot (formerly Meche's Nite Spot)

NIGHTCLUB WITH LIVE ZYDECO MUSIC ON A SPORADIC SCHEDULE

533 North Main St.
Church Point, LA
70525
(713) 618-2452

As with a lot of towns lying at the loose junctures of parish roads, there isn't much in Church Point. I wound through the dark southeast from Eunice on Highway 95, and it brought me right to my destination, as if there was nothing else out there. The Hot Spot is located near one of those highway crossings, 95 and 178, sitting almost passively beside two ramshackle hip-hop clubs, like a parent giving way to the brashness of youth. The Hot Spot looks to have its origin in the disco years; a bit of railing fences off the sunken dance floor decorated with geometric patterns in the tile.

The only reason I knew this place existed is that the mighty Keith Frank, one of the elder wizards of zydeco, was playing that night. Both a veteran and a maverick of zydeco, Frank plays the tiniest, most out-of-the-way places, little holes where zydeco is allowed to mutate and scratch out an existence. At one point during the show, Frank laid down his accordion for a break and the band launched into "I Got Loaded," the one song I hear in every sector of Louisiana culture, be it blues, Cajun, zydeco, or otherwise. Everyone can relate to the existential journey it portrays:

> Last night, I got loaded
> On a bottle of gin, on a bottle of gin
> And I feel alright
> I feel alright
> I feel alright

The narrative continues through time—night before last it was a bottle of whiskey; tonight, a

Keith Frank performing
at the Hot Spot

bottle of wine—culminating each time in joyous persistence, a willingness for another go, and that's how these old clubs and the music found therein seem to roll. The band launched into a generic slow dance and a few couples took to the floor.

At the Hot Spot, the strobe lights behind the drum kit were flickering like a fit, the laser apparatus in the corner cast green heat lightning across the ceiling, and a few lights hung over the bar and the band, but otherwise, like most zydeco clubs, it was dark and loud in there, and I took my beer to a table near the dance floor and tried to be inconspicuous. This was one of many times in the course of my visits to south Louisiana music halls that I found myself to be the only white person in a zydeco club, and I will say that I generally get treated as a curiosity at best but usually go ignored by the crowd. Zydeco audiences tend to be more self-reflective than do blues or even Cajun ones. It's not unusual for the band to be cast in the dark up on the stage; this evening Frank had a light on over his amp and mixer, but there were no stage lights highlighting the rest of the group. The band in a zydeco club is there to provide entertainment, and when people take to the floor, their attention is on each other.

Frank retook the stage and the band regained its thunder. A guy in a Drew Brees jersey instigated a dance-off with another in a cowboy hat. Brees's signature move was to fall to his knees in a squat reminiscent of when Hendrix summoned flames from his guitar, while his cowboy friend did a hyperkinetic version of the zydeco chicken strut. I don't know who won.

I do know that Frank then upped the weirdness quotient

by kicking on a sampler in his effects rack. A disembodied auto-tuned rap wove its alien way through the disco/zydeco/zydisco throb, and the corral of the dance floor started to fill up. This is why I love Keith Frank's music so much. It's rooted in tradition and family and preservation, but those roots serve to nurture the skyward-reaching branches of his art. It is world pulse music with its epicenter in backwater forgotten clubs like the Hot Spot. Neither the strobe nor the laser could keep up with the polyrhythm of it all, but all the people on the dance floor found their own part of the groove, twisting away with each other out there at a lost intersection in the dark.

Hambonz Piano Bar

UPSCALE R&B CLUB WITH SOUL MUSIC ON SPORADIC WEEKENDS

212 Railroad Ave.
Donaldsonville, LA
70346
(225) 910-3302
facebook.com/
hambonz

As I took off on a cold December night toward Donaldsonville to check out Hambonz Piano Bar, a place that calls itself "A Soulful Juke Joint," it got me thinking about soul music. Soul music is one of those genres I love but rarely will throw on. Maybe it's the immediate comfort that soul provides. It sits at a crossroads of blues and jazz and rock, smoothing down the edge of all that brought it. Soul is one of those types of music that usurps other forms and makes them gloriously its own. The sappiest, most embarrassing country ballad can be rendered glorious and glowing when a seasoned soul band gets hold of it. Soul music is where the roll gets more attention than the rock, where the vibrations that make up the music are drenched in sweat and honey and sent to invade all who listen. I thumbed through my iPod and couldn't find the soul groove I sorely needed right then, but a quick scan of my radio dial found salvation in Smokey Robinson's "Just My Imagination (Running Away with Me)," which brought about my ascension. That and the steep rise of the Sunshine Bridge.

The streets had a handful of people out despite it being bitterly cold for Louisiana. I poked my head in the Grapevine on Railroad Avenue, its resplendent dining room being where some key scenes in *All the King's Men* were filmed, hoping to catch a bit of the eclectic classical folk duo that was holding court with the stragglers, but the place was shutting down. Fortunately, the familiar slow thud of the bass drum from across the street caught my ear. It was the Flavor Band kicking into gear in the back of Hambonz.

When you get there, take a moment to look through the pileup of instruments and musical ephemera artfully stacked in the display window. A banjo and a guitar

Donaldsonville

lie over a poster for a long-forgotten show, while an old piano rests on the other side. The hodgepodge in that display case is but a taste of what you see when you venture inside. The long, narrow room spent much of its life as a shoe store before owner Darryl Hambrick purchased the place a little over five years ago. A row of tables occupies the left side, with a gorgeous long bar on the right and an aisle leading down to the informal stage area in the back where the Flavor Band has set up. The lighting in the place is simple and perfect—a row of Christmas lights runs over the tables, and some track lighting overhead bathes the room in a warm glow, as inviting as the people there.

What's also striking is that among the blues and soul artifacts set about (some borrowed from the African American Museum down the street operated by Hambrick's sister Kathe) is the number of vinyl record albums on the wall. As you move through the place, you start to notice that these records are everywhere, including sitting under a sheet of glass on the bar. Each one is covered with Day-Glo lettering and dates. Manager Juli Willis explains, "People love to come here for special events, like weddings and receptions and family reunions, and when they do, we have them sign an album and we set it up somewhere around the bar."

The club recently celebrated its fifth anniversary in style. "All the ladies wore red dresses, all the men wore ties," says Willis. This and the bar's motto, "Where Grown Folks Party," underscore the classy atmosphere at the place. Hambonz has a VIP membership that includes half off for cover and merchandise, discounts on drink specials, and special VIP nights twice a month. I was seated across from a table of VIP members who seemed to be making the most of their membership status. The beauty of the crowd there is that everyone is relaxed. Willis notes, "We get a diverse crowd in here. Donaldsonville has people from all walks of life, and the ones that come here know it's safe and they are gonna have a good time."

Right then, a member of the Flavor Band announced, "Put your hands together for the dynamic combo of Alu and Kamesha," who broke into a stellar rendition of Tyrone Davis's disco-soul classic "Turn Back the Hands of Time." A couple of people took to the impromptu dance floor in front of the band while others flitted around from barstool to table, laughing and carrying on. The vibe in the place was much like the soul music doled out by the band; everything flowed together seamlessly with all the edges smoothed over. It was one of the more relaxing bar experiences I've had. Just as I was about to brave the cold and head back to Baton Rouge, the duo launched into "Just My Imagination," bringing everything full circle for a warm night of the soul.

DETOUR:

Eunice and Swamp Pop

ajuns are a fiercely proud people, and they should be; they have one of the most vibrant and unique cultures in America, but one gets the feeling that there is a sense among them that they are not supposed to be proud. Much of this stems from the late 1800s, when English-only movements spread across the country; in 1916, state law mandated that French could no longer be spoken in public schools, and many cite that as a near fatal blow to Cajun culture. Cajun music fell from prominence and was assimilated into swamp pop, a Louisiana spin on fifties rock 'n' roll and dance hall pop.

Eunice and the surrounding area were a hotbed for this music; places like the Rendezvous Club and the Green Frog and the massive and elegant Purple Peacock, whose shell sits like a slumbering tropical bird on the outskirts of Eunice, are legendary. It's where Louisiana music had a golden age, even shone through the glare of nearby New Orleans, but it wasn't Cajun music. The culture remained dormant, almost secret.

It wasn't until the 1960s that the national Bilingual Education Act and the formation of the Council for the Development of French in Louisiana (CODOFIL) opened the doors of Cajun music. The radio broadcasts at Fred's Lounge in Mamou reintroduced it into the mainstream, and it started to flourish.

Many Cajuns I encounter remain understandably guarded about Cajun culture, having seen it assimilated into near oblivion before. Their hesitance can make it hard to find those little pockets where it still exists in its original, beautiful state. The ambassadors of Cajun culture understand that it must leave the prairie and the swamps, that it must extend its tendrils into the world for it to survive, and between those two sides a delicate balance is struck, one that can perhaps best be experienced in Eunice.

Cruiser's Tavern

SMALL, HOMEY BAR ON A LONELY STRETCH OF HIGHWAY 190

4776 Hwy. 190
Eunice, LA
70535
(337) 457-9290

I jetted out in the dark toward Eunice, listening to "Louisiana Pride" KBON. I love this station and its embrace of a most unhip mix of zydeco and swamp pop. It played Richard LeBouef's excellent version of "Take a Letter, Maria," and the DJ told a story of how LeBouef once pulled him on stage to sing this divorce ballad to impress the awestruck DJ's granddaughter.

Perched out there in the flat expanse of this part of Highway 190 is Cruiser's Tavern, a sweet little hole-in-the-wall place. I walked in, and the bartender and the only customer in the place were dancing to a zydeco song on the jukebox. I suppose I'm glad I arrived when I did, lest they were planning on taking further advantage of a slow night.

The bar has a particular clientele: the Pipeliners' Union 798. The mirror behind the bar is festooned with placards stating, "Pussies can't be pipeliners." A few of the brothers of the 798 finally trickled in, relieving me of feeling like an awkward third wheel. The bar felt more like a clubhouse then. It made me wish I had a union of resourceful co-workers who could keep a cozy little bar like this open out on the long, lonely stretches of highway through the Acadiana prairie.

Lakeview Park and Beach

FUN RV CAMPGROUND WITH SWIMMING BEACH AND LARGE BARN WITH LIVE CAJUN MUSIC EVERY FRIDAY AND SATURDAY NIGHT

1717 Veterans Memorial Hwy. (Hwy. 13)
Eunice, LA
70535
(337) 457-2881
lvpark.com/

The first thing I noticed was the baby. The baby was making some curious, unsteady motions across the concrete floor of the immense ramshackle barn at the back of the Lakeview RV Park. A young man, maybe the father, reached out to the baby, distracted by the band in the corner sawing away on fiddles, squeezing a beautiful din out of accordions, but the baby was justifiably transfixed. Couples stepped into the clockwork cycle of a Cajun waltz, careful to give the toddler a healthy berth until the young man swept the child up in his arms and joined the fray.

Things happen differently in RV parks. People who RV strike a curious balance between private and public, piloting these twenty-plus-foot mobile cabins around for weekend jaunts and summer vacations. My dad was an RV guy. Every summer we would pilot our twenty-three-footer across the plains to Colorado, up the Blue Ridge Parkway, up to places he'd been many years before with the kids from his first marriage. More often than not, we would pull into one of these places, and my dad would fall right into a rekindled friendship with someone he met at this very campground decades past, one based not on work or background or social circles but instead on simple simultaneous presence. *We are here, so let's be friends.* Some of my fondest memories are of times spent at these parks. I remember seeing a family of bears outside one park near Silverado, Colorado, the same one in which, in the post-campfire dark, among the din of tree frogs and cicadas, I managed my first real kiss off a girl from Denton, Texas, whose dad also had a taste for the mountains. What I'm saying is: you make friends fast in these places.

Compared with some of the primitive campgrounds I remember, Lakeview is pretty swank. The ninety-five tree-lined

Feufollet at the
Lakeview RV Park

sites are spread out over the forty-two-acre park, boasting free cable and wireless Internet along with the traditional power hookups. A few one-bedroom cabins are being added to the property as well. There are playgrounds, a fishing lake, a cool, fresh-water beach, even a laundry. All it is missing is a coffee shop, but then a general store is also in the works, so who knows? Lakeview really has everything, but it also has something special in its barn dances on Friday and Saturday nights.

Pulling from the rich pool of talent in the Acadiana area, the *bal de magasin* ("store dance," or in this case, barn dance) kicks off every Friday and Saturday night around 8 p.m. with a nominal cover charge. This is where I encountered the baby and crowd of seasoned travelers, skinny Lafayette hipsters, and the usual masterful Cajun dancers, all caught up in the spell of Feufollet. One of the best of the trans-traditionalist Cajun bands to come out of Lafayette in the past decade, Feufollet is the perfect band for this setting. They look young and a little hungry, channeling their young energy into songs of old, imbuing them with a modicum of ragged charm that practically blends into the clapboard walls of the barn.

The barn is a temporary home for the dances. On the property lies a dance hall measuring more than 6,000 square feet that in its prime hosted Cajun music luminaries like Ray Abshire and Dewey Balfa, and, as of this writing, the park is in the process of restoring it to its former glory. In the meantime, the barn will more than suffice. In my attempts to take in the barn's cavernous state—its rafters festooned with holiday lights make you feel like you've been swallowed by some sort of celestial whale—I accidentally stumbled right through a pair of beers that had been carefully set on the sidelines by a dancing couple. Stepping on the beer of a man and his date might be fighting words in some places I frequent, but all's good in the RV park, and so I headed to the makeshift bar in the back corner to replace them, and there, bouncing on the hip of a young woman behind the counter, was that baby again. That baby gets around.

The dance had none of the formality of the more traditional Cajun dance halls; you had the old couples who appeared to slide around as if on glass, hip kids more than ready to break out some very practiced chank-a-chank acrobatics, and some folks who just let the canned beer and convivial atmosphere put their feet in whatever motion the moment calls for. It reflected the easy mix of people that comes with RVing: homey, nuanced, and, most important, a shared temporary homeyness. The barn at Lakeview is about as sweet a place as I've been in recent memory. It made me wish my parents still had the RV so I could join in.

On my way out, the tree frogs and cicadas were competing with the band to add a musical counterpoint to the stars. A few revelers tore through the night on bikes, circling the massive bonfire roaring in the parking lot, the sweetest manifestation of drunken revelry. I wondered if some boy was out there wandering the dark with some girl from Texas when I looked back and saw that baby once again being whirled around the dance floor in the arms of a new person, perhaps in a way, in the warm embrace of everyone.

The Liberty Theater

VINTAGE PERFORMANCE HALL WITH TRADITIONAL CAJUN MUSIC EVERY SATURDAY EVENING

200 Park Ave.
Eunice, LA
70535
(337) 457-6577
eunice-la.com/
libertyschedule.html

The Liberty Theater in Eunice is a holdover from the days when every decent railroad stop had its own opera house, a glittering environ opening its arms to weary travelers to show what a town has to offer. Passenger trains don't cut through Eunice anymore, but there is rarely a bad weekend to hit the Liberty Theater. Every Saturday night at 6 p.m., the *Rendezvous Des Cajuns,* a variety show using the down-home format reminiscent of the *Grand Ole Opry* and *Louisiana Hayride* programs, broadcasts (KEUN in Eunice and KRVS in Lafayette) from its stage, attracting the finest traditional Cajun musicians around. On this particular weekend, the Louisiana Main Street program was sponsoring the world-renowned BeauSoleil with Michael Doucet in the afternoon, and later, local hero Jo-El Sonnier was appearing on the broadcast.

First, a word about the theater itself. In the twenties and thirties Eunice was a stop on the famed Rock Island railroad line, and the Keller family owned two theaters back to back, the Queen on one corner and the Liberty on the other. The Liberty was the showcase vaudeville and movie house, with the likes of Fatty Arbuckle, Roy Rogers, and Tex Ritter gracing its proscenium in its heyday. In 1987, the city of Eunice purchased the aging movie house and opened it as the Liberty Center for the Performing Arts. The mural at the back of the stage depicts the prairie Cajun life of living on the land. The interior is a gleaming example of proto-modern Chicago architecture, replete with murals designed by someone I could identify only as "old man Zelman" and breathtaking etched glass by the late Nancy Stagg. The balcony holds the camera and broadcast gear, but the real action is on the floor, where its thousand seats are frequently abandoned for the dance floor when the band starts cooking.

When I arrived, the famed ambassadors of Cajun culture

Eunice

BeauSoleil avec Michael Doucet had just taken the stage. In most parts of the world, if people have heard Cajun music firsthand, chances are it was emanating from Doucet's fiddle. Their performance was the final stop on a tour of Louisiana Main Street communities called "Thirty Years of BeauSoleil avec Michael Doucet," where the band brought their impeccable musicianship and knowledge of the culture to theaters all across the state.

Doucet is a virtuoso of the droning double-string style most Cajun musicians employ and the darker, deeper Eastern European style, where the violin transcends being merely an instrument and opens a conduit to the hereafter. Doucet explained BeauSoleil's approach to music making during the Q&A session in the middle of the concert, stating they aim to "show the subtlety in our music, the ballads, the Tin Pan Alley favorites adapted to this style, not just the two-steps and waltzes." An older woman in the audience took issue with Doucet, citing the banishing of French in the schools as a factor that brought in these wider influences, but Doucet countered politely by demonstrating the pan-European influences in the music, the influence of 1950s country music, and Cajun music's influence on it, namely, Hank Williams's biggest hit, "Jambalaya," and so on. I'm not sure the woman was convinced that Doucet was doing the right thing, but I did notice that she was among the couples who got up to dance once he stopped talking and started playing again.

This is what I like about BeauSoleil; they don't treat Cajun music like a museum piece that needs to be delicately handled but rather as a vibrant, living form of music with roots in all the music of the world. I like how they believe that this music is strong enough to weather both the forces of the outside world and the sometimes restrictive traditions from within.

I had a little time to kill between the BeauSoleil show and the radio performance, so I sauntered down Park Avenue to take in the Cajun Music Hall of Fame—and a wealth of artifacts and photos from the history of Cajun music in the prairie parishes. Old records, accordions, instruments, and a wall of photos give a glimpse at the place in history that Cajun music holds.

This stop of the Main Street Project had manifested itself into a small street fair—if you've ever been to Eunice during Mardi Gras, you'd understand that street festivals are something for which Eunice has a marked proclivity. Russ Chenier and the Inner City Band were set up on a flatbed stage in a parking lot across the street from the theater, playing blues and R&B to a motorcycle club taking advantage of the beautiful weather. Chenier's throbbing blues and the accompanying barbeque pork sandwiches were a perfect afternoon lagniappe.

I still had a couple of hours to kill before Jo-El Sonnier's appearance at the theater, so I popped into the library across the street to check email. Soon enough, though, one of the librarians peered through the blinds and remarked, "They sure are lining up out there." A line had formed around the block for Jo-El Sonnier's performance that night, and I had neglected to get a ticket early, so I logged out to join the fray.

I had just walked in to catch BeauSoleil that afternoon and didn't anticipate having to queue up a full hour and a half before the performance was set to start. I asked a woman who joined the line behind me if the line was always this long, and she said with a smirk, "If the performers are good, it is. I bet they didn't have a line like this for Michael Doucet." I asked her what was wrong with Michael Doucet. "I respect what he does," she offered, masking her condescension, "going around the world and all, but no, I prefer the more traditional style."

Jo-El Sonnier has laid his own tracks outside Acadiana. Born to French-speaking sharecroppers in Rayne, he took to the accordion before his tenth birthday and had his first recording session at eleven. After becoming a local club sensation in young adulthood, he headed off to California, where he found success as a session musician. In the mid-seventies his solo country music career took off in Nashville, including a contract with Mercury and a stint as Merle Haggard's opening act. In the mid-eighties, he found himself a foothold in the neotraditionalist country movement along with Albert Lee and Emmylou Harris. He had a couple of top-ten country hits, including "No More One More Time" and a version of English folk-rock icon Richard Thompson's "Tear-Stained Letter" that reciprocated the Cajun inspiration with which Thompson wrote the song and, in a sense, brought it back home. Jo-El Sonnier has performed with Elvis Costello and Edie Brickell and has even acted in a few movies. I wanted to explain to the woman in line that Sonnier performed on a number of BeauSoleil's albums in the nineties, but this was her tradition to parameterize, not mine. Eventually, it was his love of and talent at the Cajun accordion that formed the cohesive thread through Jo-El Sonnier's career, with albums named *Cajun Life* (for which he received a Grammy nomination), *Cajun Pride, Cajun Blood,* and, concurrent with this appearance, the self-released *The Real Deal.*

Sonnier's traditional Cajun music is powerful and percussive, filling every crevasse of the theater with reels of fiddle and accordion. During his first numbers, the crowd was mesmerized by his dexterity on the accordion, playing it with the bravado and power of a lead guitarist. But when the band launched into a rousing two-step, the audience left the seats, forming a circle of dancers that exhibited a precision Swiss clockmakers would find enviable. There is nothing better than watching older Cajun couples dance; the group synchronization is almost kaleidoscopic. This mix of movement and powerful music was eclipsed only by the thunderclap of applause when the song finished. The group continued with a cycle of waltzes and two-steps and jump country tunes, intermixed with half-French, half-English commentary from the announcer. It didn't matter to me or anyone else in attendance where Jo-El Sonnier had gone in his life or what he sought for himself out there; it was the fact that he was here and now along with us in this majestic room, in the cycle of dancers and listeners and ambassadors and locals, an embodiment of Cajun music's enduring wonder.

Nick's on 2nd

LARGE VINTAGE BAR WITH GENEROUS DANCE FLOOR; CAJUN AND ZYDECO BANDS MOST SATURDAY NIGHTS AND EVERY SUNDAY AFTERNOON

123 South Second St.
Eunice, LA
70535
(337) 457-4921
nickson2nd.com/

Just a block or so down from the Liberty Theater lies another extant Eunice tradition—Nick's, a massive place with a courtyard filled with the pleasantly inebriated abutting the serpentine parking lot that is downtown Eunice's main drag. I like how Cajun people pass a good time. There is a lot of jostling in the glut of folks on the patio, loud laughter, a perpetuity of greetings and good-byes as you navigate around them to get in the bar. They are almost like teenagers, fully engaged with their connections. Inside, more crowds coalesce around the tables. One extended African American family toward the back has a few tables pulled together with balloons and a massive cake for a birthday party, the strapping sons posted at the end in cowboy hats as if standing watch. I see a heavy-set guy in immaculate snakeskin loafers guide a beautiful younger woman onto the dance floor as the bride-to-be cuts behind them over to where I am stationed by the bar.

I call her the bride-to-be because she is wearing a plastic tiara with a fluffy gauze veil billowing out, though she had some sort of pink sash on, so it's possible that it was simply her birthday or she'd been elected the queen of some Louisiana agricultural product that evening. Regardless, she and her crew were having a party, and her veil was pulled to the back so she could do a tequila shot. The bartender had to explain the deal with the salt and the lemon, so I'm guessing some important bridge in her life was being freshly crossed, and Nick's seems a great place to do it.

The gorgeous ornate bar dates from the opening of Nick's in 1937. Before then, there was a second floor that served as a speakeasy during Prohibition. Now the club boasts a cathedral ceiling decked out in elegant painted tin over the dance floor. That night, Geno Delafose and French Rockin' Boogie had

Eunice

Geno Delafose and the
Rockin' Boogie at Nick's

the place, well, rockin'. For as long as I can remember, Geno and his crew have stood as the hardest-working band on the Cajun/zydeco circuit, sometimes seemingly omnipresent. There have been days when I've seen them play at an afternoon festival and encountered them later that evening in another town on my bar hop home. Geno's music is like a Venn diagram of Louisiana culture, each tune a flawlessly rendered combination of Cajun, zydeco, country, and blues. He's the logical extension of the great Clifton Chenier, who could channel any and all music through his accordion no matter where he was hired.

At Geno's shows, it is common to see the white Cajun audiences and black zydeco crowds come together in the same place. As the bride-to-be and her girlfriends staggered out on the dance floor, so did couples from a Creole family gathering at a table near the bar. Geno gave a Marvin Gaye tune his pan-Louisiana treatment and the room swayed into step. Black men in cowboy hats made the circle with older white couples in matching Hawaiian shirts and even the errant mixed-race couple thrown in. It was a beautiful reminder that while racial tensions persist throughout Louisiana culture, a separation that plays out on a checkerboard of predominantly white and predominantly black clubs, there are some places where the lines get blurry.

Savoy Music Center

MUSIC STORE SPECIALIZING IN CAJUN ACCORDIONS; LIVE CAJUN MUSIC JAM ON
SATURDAY MORNINGS

Hwy. 190, between
Eunice and Lawtell, LA
(337) 457-9563
savoymusiccenter.com/

Marc Savoy has been playing, building, and selling Acadian accordions out of the Savoy Music Center—located on Highway 190 between Lawtell and Eunice—since 1960, and every Saturday morning from nine to noon he hosts a Cajun music jam. I emailed ahead to make sure the center was having one so soon after the New Year, and I was told: "You are welcome to come and do your story, but don't forget the price of admission—a pound of boudin or a six-pack of beer—or both."

Fortunately, the best places to get boudin, or an emergency six-pack for that matter, are the service stations between Breaux Bridge and Eunice. Boudin is a loose sausage of pork, liver, and rice in natural casing with as many recipes as there are gas stations selling it. I don't know why a gas station is the right venue for this dish, but it is. I spied a big red sign declaring BOUDIN from one of the exits right before Lafayette. The first batch was already in the steam tray this early in the morning, and my car was consumed with the spicy, earthy aroma as I made my way up I-49 to Opelousas and then west on Highway 190 to the Savoy.

The directions on the website read, "If you're wondering how to find the music center, just look for thirty cars lined up Hwy. 190," and it couldn't have been more accurate. I pulled in behind a mammoth RV and walked past a hundred yards of cars with my Styrofoam clamshell of boudin in hand. The music center is a large green house set just off the highway in the mass expanse of a rice field. Most of the week, it serves as the place where Marc Savoy makes and sells Cajun accordions. When Marc was a kid, a neighboring farmer introduced him to the instrument, and soon he got his own from a Sears catalog. One of the springs broke, and once he repaired it with a safety pin as his father said older musicians had done, he embarked on

Eunice

Jam session at the Savoy
Music Center

a lifetime of perfecting the instrument and, through that, strengthening the musical traditions that flow through its bellows. A crowd of about thirty was assembled in rows in front of a circle of musicians in full swing. I whispered to one of the people behind the counter, "I was told to bring boudin," and he responded, "Looks like you take orders well," pointing me to the other decimated Styrofoam trays of the stuff on the counter.

The music was heavenly. Most of the times I hear Cajun music, it is in the service of the dance floor, where a crowd is looking for familiar precise two-steps and waltzes to which they can demonstrate their prowess, but this session was for playing and listening. Anchored by an accordion and a triangle— "Please, no more than one triangle player at a time" is requested on the website—and bolstered by an exquisite pedal steel, a circle of guitarists and fiddlers worked through classics of the Cajun repertoire. With that many players, though, these pieces built on economy and precision took on an ethereal, cosmic quality.

The attending musicians were tight, and like any great jam session, the solos shifted around the circle wordlessly and effortlessly, as if they were clouds passing the blue of the sky. With that many players playing the rhythm, a natural choirlike delay blurs the edges of the songs into becoming an angelic chorus, a beautiful noise like the wind blowing through trees. It is not often you get to hear a phalanx of acoustic guitars and accordions playing the same melody, with a fiddle section in

SAVOY MUSIC CENTER

81

accompaniment, but it is an amazing thing. The acoustics in the music center are perfect for this informal splendor—with more echo, the magic would disperse. Just as I was being transported by this rattling choir, the serpentine pedal steel would sneak in with its honey-dripping glow. It made me rethink my perception of Cajun music, allowing it to stretch beyond the bounds of the dance band and the cultural relic struggling to persist against the tide of modernity. It revealed itself to be beautiful, flexible, and timeless.

Marc Savoy is more than an instrument builder and a musician; he's a cultural philosopher with formidable wit and insight. On one of the many hand-lettered broadsides posted around the room, he explains his "General Theory of Cultural Relativity."

> The difficulty in comprehending the subtleties that
>   account for its uniqueness,
> Resulting in the exaggeration of what is obvious because
>   the subtleties aren't recognized,
> Together with the near impossibility of articulating the
>   subtleties once they are understood.

Wrapping one's brain around that is like wrapping one's taste buds around a link of boudin. The seemingly simple ingredients are combined in such idiosyncratic ways that you get so taken with contrasts between Cajun culture and the rest of the country that you lose sight of the subtle differences that shape the Cajun way of life. It's easy to fall into a "noble savage" trap with Cajun culture, to read its reticence for assimilation as stubbornness or even ignorance when, like in the old Cajun songs cycling through the air of this little accordion shop on the highway, the forces at play must be in motion for the right balance to be maintained.

Angelle's Whiskey River Landing

WATERFRONT BAR; CAJUN AND ZYDECO MUSIC EARLY SUNDAY EVENINGS

1365 Henderson Levee Rd.
Henderson, LA
70517
(337) 228-2277
whiskeyriverlanding.net/

Technically, Angelle's Whiskey River Landing is on the south tip of Lake Bigeaux, at a point dubbed Cypremort Crevasse, but for all intents and purposes, this is the mythical Whiskey River our friend Willie with the braids sings about—Angelle's serves as a port of call for motorboats and party barges to depart for a drunken, lazy afternoon in the swamp.

I like a place off the beaten path, but it's rare that I end up at a place you can't even see from the road—once you hang a right by the landmark lighthouse at Pat's Fisherman's Wharf, a wooden sign leads you up on a gravel road over the levee to Angelle's insular world. Cars and campers are strewn in loose order on the grass surrounding the small club. An airboat was sitting in its trailer behind a white pickup near the wooden porch at the entrance. I don't know if I've come up with a magic formula that would indicate how fun a place is from the outside, but I can safely say that the presence of an airboat in the parking lot is a good sign. As I marveled at it, a guy in his fifties with an inspiring silver Aqua Net helmet of hair and a waxed moustache said, "Y'all come on in."

Angelle's is basically a gargantuan screened back porch attached to the bar. Jeffery Broussard & the Creole Cowboys were playing on a stage on the water side, grinding away that familiar zydeco stomp groove under a wooden sign that had WHISKEY RIVER spelled out in holiday lights. For something as down home as this place was, it was rather fabulous. The dance floor ebbed and flowed with each number as couples made their way around the room, igniting the air with swamp-fueled libido.

"People come out here to party, where there's not going to be any trouble," said Don Brasseaux, a furniture maker

Henderson

Jeffery Broussard & the Creole Cowboys at Angelle's Whiskey River Landing

from Breaux Bridge and expert Cajun dancer. He also was a bartender at Whiskey River Landing back before it was a dance hall. "This was a swamp bar, and this covered deck was used for weigh-ins for fishing tournaments. Sometime in the early nineties, the bandstand was added and the porch was screened in, and the dance hall took off." He confirmed that a lot of single people come out here to meet other people in a relaxed, fun atmosphere and that folks wander in to continue the party after an afternoon on the rented barges. "There's a lot of freedom without it being a free-for-all."

The moment that got me was when one of the rousing numbers from Jeffery Broussard slowly transformed into a gospel roll, just the accordion and washboard, punctuated by a stomp from the kick drum. It was an amalgamation of Sunday tradition, sacred and profane, that had the room clapping, dancing, and rejoicing on a cypress porch out in the swamp, people of all ages, races, and states of inebriation coming together in this one place for a glorious moment. It seemed to me that this is what Sunday should really be about.

Throughout the afternoon, rented party barges lazily deposit their sunburned, half-drunk occupants on the dock, and they cover up enough to join the fray inside. I was hoping to be in the right place and time for the owner of the airboat to offer to take me screaming across the vastness of the Atchafalaya, but no dice. The sacrament at Whiskey River reaches a fever pitch as the evening takes hold and the crowd gets looser. At last call, it's a tradition at Angelle's that the ladies in the house get up and dance the final number up on the bar. They have a T-shirt for sale saying you did it. It becomes its own circus when accordions, wobbly barstools, and even wobblier women in dancing heels navigate such daring heights in their state, but the night I was there, everyone survived and the cars started disappearing over the crest of the levee destined for parts unknown.

McGee's Landing Inc.

WATERSIDE RESTAURANT WITH RENTAL CABINS; CAJUN MUSIC ON SUNDAYS

1337 Henderson
Levee Rd.
Henderson, LA
70517
(337) 228-2384
mcgeeslanding.com

The Atchafalaya begs a sort of contemplative mood, even from the car on either of the seemingly endless elevated highways traversing it. I'm often struck with wondering why anyone ever decided to go this way, spend all this money and effort just to get across the swamp. Once I'm out there, though, with those cypress knees poking through the surface and those forlorn trees standing out on the serene yet surreal infinitude of water, I can't help but wonder why you wouldn't head this way.

The levee is dotted with landings serving just that wandering spirit. McGee's Landing offers guest cabins sitting in piers and is the dock for guided basin tours. The restaurant serves better-than-average Cajun fare, and on Sundays at noon, low-key Cajun acts play in the bar overlooking the water. McGee's is a wonderfully tranquil experience, a breather between the hectic complex at Pat's Fisherman's Wharf and the mayhem just down the levee at Angelle's Whiskey River Landing. Last time I went, my buddy Clarke and I were serenaded by an accordion and fiddle duo as we dug into our poboys at the bar, the sole audience for their informal set. In their defense, the Saints were working their way to the playoffs that afternoon, and we tried not to make it too obvious that our attention was on the TV behind the bar. Even the band started packing up when the game got good.

Hende

Pat's Fisherman's Wharf & Atchafalaya Club

MASSIVE RESTAURANT, HOTEL, AND DANCE HALL; CAJUN MUSIC ON THE WEEKENDS

1008 Henderson
Levee Rd.
Henderson, LA
70517
(337) 228-7512
patsfishermanswharf.com/

Baton Rouge's draconian blue laws on Sundays sent the less repentant souls of the flock scurrying to the swamps, across the I-10 bridge into the wilds of the Atchafalaya to the curious pocket of civilization that is Henderson. Upon landing, Henderson doesn't look like much as you snake past the gas stations and the McDonalds. Head down Highway 352 and the promises don't appear any firmer. There are signs of failed or failing competition on the road that takes you from the Henderson exit off I-10 down to the crook of the road that veers off down the levee—a sign for what looks to have once been a massive, generically named Zydeco Dance Hall and Restaurant, something called the Party Zone; it's tough keeping a business going literally out in the middle of the swamp. Across unassuming Bayou Amy to the base of the levee, the monstrous complex that is Pat's Fisherman's Wharf weirdly thrives. It was so crowded on this one Sunday night that I had to park my car on a rather steep slope near the levee road, hoping it wouldn't tumble into one of the hundreds of cars choking the gravel lot that snakes between the two restaurants, the hotel, the giant lighthouse out front, the sugar mill with the water wheel spinning away the years, since it might have actually been part of a sugar mill. Pat's has an alligator pond and a deck around the circumference of the complex that offers a breathtakingly lazy panorama of the swamp.

A man named Henry Guidry moved his restaurant and dance hall to the area in 1934 when the levees stabilized the flooding of the Atchafalaya. He eventually sold that business to Pat Huval, who started with a hamburger and crawfish stand near the train tracks and built not only a business but a town as well. When Henderson incorporated in 1971, Huval was elected mayor the next year and held that position for seventeen years.

The Atchafalaya Club

Pat's Fisherman's Wharf is a culmination of his vision, his *Gesamtkunstwerk,* and at the core of this complex is the Atchafalaya Club, perhaps the most glamorous joint in the swamp area.

It is shocking that a place this big is effectively tucked away even in a massive compound like Pat's, but the dimensional shock upon entering is not only one of space but one of time as well. The back wall of the building is frescoed with the requisite swamp mural that you find throughout Acadiana establishments, except this one is actually as big as the real swamp while across from it sits an ornate art deco bar lined with plush red leather seats and lit by a trio of sparkling chandeliers. Walk a hundred paces in and you'll find a second bar just like it. A nearly infinite line of tables with chairs matching the bar leads up to the dance floor at the center and the stage where bands have been drawing audiences for decades.

The Sunday afternoon I went, High Performance was commanding the stage. On name alone, you might mistake this group for just a variety band or possibly a swamp pop outfit, but High Performance is about something deeper. It is a resurrection of a faded musical tradition, armed with not-so-secret weapons: pedal steel maestro Richard Comeaux and accordionist and leader of the world-renowned Mamou Playboys, Steve Riley. High Performance was dreamed up as a way to recapture the Nashville influence on Cajun dance bands in the 1960s; two-steps lent a glissando daydream from pedal steel, amped up by a twin-fiddle assault. It is not the way Cajun music is "traditionally" played but instead part of its past reality. Upon hearing the group's high-octane take on it, you are left wondering if it shouldn't be played this way more often.

The elegant swoop of the pedal steel and the old-timey glitz of the club open a time door to a rich past, when these Sunday night dances were the reward for the previous six days of the week. Couples darted around the floor like it was a skating rink, jitterbugs and fancy footwork weaving in with the clockwork two-steppers. Befitting the nature of High Performance's music, the dancing was adrenalized, inspiring the occasional show-off. I have to think this cutting loose has something to do with being out here in the swamp, away from the day to day.

I walked outside to the gator pond, adjacent to the restaurant, and stood with a gaggle of kids momentarily fleeing the tyranny of a sit-down family meal, hoping to cajole one of the slumbering beasts to snap to the surface, but they wouldn't give. Alligators are not known for their cooperation. The better sights are just around the corner on the walkway circling the back side of the club. Look off to the west and a traffic bridge looms almost like a silhouette cutting across the sunset and lushness of the swamp at twilight. A fisherman glides slowly by as I look east, and the slight eddies are undulating folds on the fabric of nature, dyed blue by the sky. A couple on the far end of the walkway pause, hand in hand, to take in this most romantic view of the swamp.

Jolly Inn

TRADITIONAL CAJUN RESTAURANT AND DANCE HALL; LIVE CAJUN MUSIC ON FRIDAY
AND SUNDAY EVENINGS

1507 Barrow St.
Houma, LA
70360
(985) 872-6114

Houma is a city that has seen its fair share of fluctuation in the past twenty years, and by the looks of Martin Luther King Boulevard, dotted with every big box store and even a Starbucks, the city seems to have finally grown past its reputation as the town that sprouted out of the cane fields. Fortunately, a few people in the city have seen the cultural erosion that tends to run with sprawl and rapid commercial development and have done some things to maintain its uniqueness. Houma is the last big city before you dive into the heart of Cajun country—and by Cajun, I mean the hunting and fishing Cajuns of the swamp as opposed to the agricultural Cajuns of the Lafayette area. It's a distinction any proud Cajun in Terrebonne Parish is quick to make.

Werlien Prosperie, proprietor of the Jolly Inn in Houma and accordionist for its house band, Couche Couche, is one of those proud Cajuns. "I was born in a houseboat down in Montegut," he says as he points out a replica of it hanging on the wall of his restaurant/dance hall. "I wasn't born on the bayou, I was born in it." For a man in his sixties, Prosperie has lost none of his fire, as evidenced when he talks about his business, which he opened in 1998. "It's like having a place where you can get a metamorphosis to back to where you came from. Used to be when someone was from the bayou and they'd move away, they'd be hesitant to say where they were from. Now they are proud to be from here."

The restaurant sits in a converted oil field warehouse, once owned by the Bethlehem Oil Company. Its hard wood floors, lofty ceiling with open rafters, and long tables bring the atmosphere of "the camp"—the many fishing and hunting retreats that the Cajuns maintain out in the swamps—into a place where tourists can, as regular Janice Leblanc put it, "experience all the

Houma

great Cajun traditions in one family-friendly place—from food to music and dance."

The kitchen in the back serves up the full menu of area seafood, from delectable shrimp poboys to heaping fried-catfish platters, but the real draw here is Prosperie's band, Couche Couche, and the chance to strut your stuff on the dance floor. Prosperie has played in various Cajun, rock, and country bands since an early age, claiming, "I was on the floors of Club Belvedere during the war at age nine." But his true love is letting the real music of the Cajuns shine through. "Music is a salvation, the deepest part of my soul. It's where I retreat to feel peace in my life." He says, "You will get producers in the big cities that will tell you what to play and how to play it, but here, we've been playing this music all our lives. I know how it's played, because I'm the one that's been playing it."

In its Friday night and Sunday afternoon concerts, Couche Couche (featuring Ronnie Filce on guitar, Norman LeBoeuf on bass, Craig Babin on fiddle, and Wilbert Foret on drums) harkens back to the bands like that of Prosperie's grandparents, who would go on a *veillé,* visiting house parties by boat to play music. "Music was not a thing we aspired to, it was a part of life. It was a thing you did along the way."

The second the band starts playing, couples both young and old hit the dance floor. You have seasoned dancers who glide around the floor like figure skaters mixing with novices who are enticed to give the two-step a try. "There are no lessons here," says Prosperie. "People just jump right in." Tourists are also invited to come up on stage and give the *frottoire* (washboard) and the *t-fer* (triangle) a try, once they get swept up in the Jolly Inn's inviting atmosphere. Prosperie explains the generosity like this: "Cajuns love to share, and even though we don't have a lot of material things to give, we share our culture with people all around the world." A glance at the guest book with addresses from all over the country and comments by people saying they can't believe how friendly everyone is will testify to this.

Regular dancer and KLEB disk jockey Gloria "Cajun Queen"

Fonseca makes the trip from Larose twice a week to dance. "It's a pretty unique place," she says. "It's very rustic yet very family oriented. You see everyone dancing with each other young and old and having a great time. My husband and I have been coming here since when they still had sawdust on the floor."

The Blue Moon Saloon & Guesthouse

SHABBY–CHIC B&B WITH CAJUN, ZYDECO, AND ROOTS ROCK BANDS
THURSDAY–SATURDAY NIGHTS

215 East Convent St.
Lafayette, LA
70501
(337) 234-2422
1-877-766-BLUE (2583)
(toll-free)
bluemoonpresents.com

I always get a little lost in Lafayette. The major streets, subtitled in French on their signs, hang off I-10 and U.S. 90 like threads woven into an idea of a town, or rather a town formed into an idea that Lafayette is, without much argument, the capital of the lost land of Acadiana. It is an urban cradle in which the fragile Cajun culture, best suited for life in the country, can thrive and mutate like any living culture must.

The Blue Moon is tucked away in a sleepy neighborhood catty-corner to the Borden's Ice Cream store, and one might drive right past it were it not for the cars choking the street and the congenial racket rattling from the back porch. The house that is now the club was moved from down the street by mules in the early 1900s to make way for the Gordon Hotel and served as a family home and flower shop until it opened for business in 2002. Since then, the Blue Moon has become a multifaceted home base for new Lafayette music. Part guest house, the Blue Moon has seven rooms ranging from shabby-chic B&B-style private accommodations (minus the breakfast) to shared rooms with single bunks, perfect for that wise decision to not venture out on the road home with people as intoxicated as yourself. The rates run from $18 for a hostel bunk to $90 for the cozy balcony room (higher rates apply during Mardi Gras and the many festivals in Lafayette), and considering a free ticket to the show (usually around $10) and a beer ticket for the bar, it really pays for itself. I imagine with the right amount of "party logic" you can come out ahead on the deal.

No food is sold at Blue Moon, though many nights there is a guy with a hot dog cart available to tickle your culinary fancy, and the bar and the band are on the back porch. Festooned with weathered

Chubby Carrier and the Bayou Swamp Band at the Blue Moon

signs and concert posters, the covered bare wood porch and bar approach true honky-tonk patina. The Blue Moon is as cozy as old shoes, even though it's a little awkward to get from the dance floor through the crowd, down the steps to the bar, and then in line for the bathrooms off the patio. I have seen many a patron stagger through that very circuit all night long.

The Blue Moon attracts a younger crowd than most Cajun bars, and a lot of that has to do with a little architecture. The back porch does have a small dance floor, but determined dancers will find them-selves pushing against the crowd watching the band, for Blue Moon is more set up like a rock club and the bands that play there command rock club attention. This per-haps is a reason for the success of the club and the neo-Cajun bands that gravitate around it: Lost Bayou Ramblers, Feufol-let, Cedric Watson, and the like. These bands are all steeped in Cajun heritage, even playing Cajun music, but had it on the back burner and only in their teenage years realized how fun the old folks music could be when injected with a little hor-monal rock 'n' roll.

Lost Bayou Ramblers are one of the groups most closely as-sociated with the bar. Brothers Andre and Louis Michot are the sons and grandsons and great-grandsons of Cajun musicians, having played in their family band, Les Freres Michot, while playing rock music on the side. Once, they brought their rock drummer friends into a practice and saw what happened when you muscled up the fiddle and accordion. They are often spoken of as the most punk rock of the young Lafayette Cajun bands.

One afternoon I was at a party in Baton Rouge where Calico, a charming female folk duo from Lafayette, was playing when my buddy Clarke texted me, "Gordon Gano is playing with Lost

Bayou Ramblers at Blue Moon tonight." Gordon Gano was the lead singer of 1980s folk-punk upstarts Violent Femmes. The pairing made perfect sense. I suddenly needed to hear "Gone Daddy Gone" with accordions and fiddles, so we took to our devices, confirmed the event, and formed a caravan that basically tailed Calico back to wonderful Lafayette, where things like that happen.

El Sid O's

OLD URBAN ZYDECO NIGHTCLUB; ZYDECO BANDS ON SPORADIC SCHEDULE

1523 North St. Antoine
Lafayette, LA
70501
(337) 235-0647

Like I said, when out in Lafayette, I generally find myself careening through those curvy Francophonized byways, on the way to some weirdly thriving touchstone to the past, and around one of those bends (St. Antoine and Martin Luther King) lies El Sid O's Zydeco and Blues Club, one of the last great zydeco clubs. Sid Williams has operated the place since 1984. His brother Nathan Williams (of Nathan and the Zydeco Cha-Cha's), now one of the great neotraditionalist zydeco frontmen who keep this music close to its roots, grew up around the place.

El Sid O's, like most of the zydeco clubs I've been to, has a darkened dance floor at its center with clusters of tables bunched up around either side. The ebb and flow between the dance floor and the tables is as hypnotic as the dancing itself; the crowds seem to bubble up just like the music does and then dissipate as the song goes out, eventually reaching a symbiosis. The stage is even darker, it seems; its red lights resemble those of a darkroom.

The night I went, just as the 2010 spring heat was about to saturate into summer, zydeco titan Keith Frank was appearing. If there is anyone that embodies the evolution of zydeco, it's Frank. Two years ago when I saw him at Slim's Y-Ki-Ki in Opelousas, his sound was a bucking bronco, whoops and hollers and his infectious groove. This time, things seemed boiled down to the essence. His washboard player stood like an armored sentry in front of two drummers with full kits. The bass was ratcheted up to deafening levels, and the guitarist ran a tight funky clothesline above it all on which Frank hung his accordion licks. That resounding thud beat is a marked part of the modern practice of zydeco, a jarring eruption like that of subwoofers in a beat-up car, momentarily rattling the universe to remind you it's there, but that night, the

Couple dancing at
El-Sid-O's

thud had taken over. It's like the transformation from reggae into dub, an amplification of basic elements that only serves to illustrate the power of the original.

The bar at El Sid O's is off to the right, with Sid looking resplendent in cowboy gear. The older crowd congregates on this side to take in the shadowy spectacle over on the darkened floor. As I tried to make my way over to a display case on the wall, I nearly tripped over a walker. A woman in her sixties was trying to get to the bathroom when she got dragged out onto an open spot on the floor by a man of similar vintage. Her friends cackled about it behind her as she cut her portion of the rug, but Keith Frank is prone to doing very long songs, and she eventually broke free from the man's orbit.

The glass reliquary was full of artifacts: a Clifton Chenier promo photo, one of his singles on the King Snake label, as well as weathered Polaroids of the bar in years past. The woman with the walker smiled as I edged past, grateful that I didn't kick it over again, and I caught my image in mirrored panels on the back wall. It was like looking into history in reverse. Many of the older patrons might have been in some of those Polaroids had they shown up on the right night. They'd perhaps been to one of Sid's big Thanksgiving Day throwdowns. Just past the tables, a gaggle of men in varying degrees of zydeco plumage stood. One had a matching black western shirt and jeans riveted up with silver studs against white boots and a hat; he would've fit right in a Parliament photo shoot. Another had a black T-shirt with an airbrushed skeleton on a motorcycle and DEATH RIDER in a bold Gothic font. Zydeco is just as much a curious sartorial art as it is a music.

Past them were the young folks, men in less exaggerated hats and baggy shirts, writhing and jerking around the dance floor.

The real interesting thing about dancing at zydeco clubs is that it's less an intimacy between couples, not the organized array in Cajun dance halls, and more organic, more slyly competitive, somewhere between a dance-off and a mating ritual. As the throngs writhed in the dark, Frank announced there were T-shirts for sale. "These are gonna be collector's items soon," he chuckled as he left the stage playing stray licks on his accordion via a wireless connection, taking in the legacy that he'd inherited from the guys in the glass case and that he was about to pass on to the next generation.

Grant Street Dance Hall

SPACIOUS OLD DANCE HALL WITH A LOT OF HISTORY; CAJUN AND ROOTS ROCK ON
SEMIREGULAR SCHEDULE

113 West Grant St.
Lafayette, LA
70501
(337) 237-8513

To this day, the Grant Street Dance Hall building still resembles the fruit warehouse it was a century before it became one of the lynchpin nightclubs for Cajun and zydeco in 1980. The foot-high stage juts out into the wide open dance floor like a gentle interruption in the dialogue between the bands and the dancers. Back in those early years, the warehouse was without air-conditioning, and opening the loading dock door behind the band to the still summer evening air offered little respite, but fortunately the place has been modified to contemporary comforts, as has the music.

Like Cajun music in recent years, Grant Street has renewed its embrace of its roots. In the middle of the first decade of this century, Grant Street capitulated to downtown Lafayette's healthy nightclub scene, hosting hip-hop shows and dance nights. In 2010, the nightclub had a reopening that was more of a statement of purpose, pulling in national touring roots rock bands and young Cajun bands, eager to edge Grant Street back into its place in Cajun culture.

I reacquainted myself with a double bill of the Pine Leaf Boys and Steve Riley & the Mamou Playboys, two bands that embody the scope of Cajun culture while understanding that it needs to be stretched to survive in the greater American culture. Steve Riley was grinding out his last number, as if he were squeezing the essence left from so many great performances in that room through his accordion to attain its essence. The second the band finished, the people on the dance floor spun out toward the bar opposite the stage, and I spied Riley over in the corner talking to swamp blues impresario C. C. Adcock. The two are members of the pan-Louisiana supergroup Lil' Band o' Gold,

which effortlessly blends swamp pop, Cajun, zydeco, and the blues into a delicious cocktail. My favorite song they do is ELO's "Hold on Tight"—I was so sure that it was some old swamp pop tune that the song was half over before I realized that it was a cover. I considered injecting myself into their narrative or at least snagging an interview, but it struck me that Grant Street is where guys like them and guys who inspired them all hung out; it was like setting up a hunting blind at the watering hole.

The Pine Leaf Boys set up in short order, and the audience spun back out to the floor. It's been a joy watching them continue to grow. The first time I saw them, they wore their Cajun heritage like a badge of honor, digging up old forgotten waltzes and two-steps from their parents' and grandparents' treasure troves of songs (accordionist Wilson Savoy is the son of Eunice's Marc Savoy; fiddler Courtney Granger is related to the Balfa family), performing them with the ardor of young idealists. Five years later, they have the rhythms of Cajun culture in their pulse and know every turn in the music's backwaters but have loosened up a little.

I was struck most by one extended two-step: it was one of those that rise and fall like an endless tide, the cyclical nature of the song drilling into your brain, when suddenly the weather shifted. The drums and the bass got heavier, trading locomotive rattle in for the steps of Godzilla emerging from the swamp. Savoy had traded off to the fiddle and extracted an arabesque out of the tune, the cymbals now stinging the air like wasps. They had gone from chank-a-chank into Led Zeppelin territory in a matter of bars, and just as you expected that loading dock door to slide open for Robert Plant to appear (Plant has done a show with Lil' Band o' Gold in New Orleans before), the band zips the diversion right back into the two-step, as if the interlude was a passing moment. The dancers, of course, hadn't lost a step in the process, but for me standing on the sidelines, it was like the breadth of the past four decades was swept up in Cajun music's embrace.

The other moment that knocked me out was not a Cajun

tune at all, but Granger handing off his fiddle to wrench out a heartbreaking version of the George Jones hit "She Thinks I Still Care." I grew up around Cajun people south of Houma, people who took their "Cajunness" with guarded seriousness, but by and large, they didn't listen to Cajun music. The young people listened to the same Ozzy Osbourne records I did, and the older folks muttered in French around the dinner table with classic country on the radio. The down-the-bayou Cajuns I knew held the Lafayette "Acadians" in suspicion, regarded them as uppity, but Granger's faithful rendition of old George would have quelled their concerns.

Classic country and Cajun music orbit each other like binary stars. Hank Williams's 1952 hit "Jambalaya (On the Bayou)" is based on the melody of an old Cajun tune, "Grand Texas," and is perhaps Cajun culture's all-time most effective ambassador to the world. Likewise, Williams was the undisputed star of the 1950s, and every Cajun musician, every blues musician, every musician of any kind from that era wanted to be him.

The band swung through "She Thinks I Still Care" like a breeze and leaped right into a majestic, artfully wrought waltz. I thought about all the performers who have played in that room, not just Louisiana legends like Clifton Chenier and Red Beans and Rice Revue, but John Lee Hooker, Jerry Lee Lewis, and Los Lobos up through the Pine Leaf Boys and the other young Cajun bands that use that low stage in Lafayette as a springboard with the dance floor full of people ready to catch them, no matter how far a jump they make.

Prejean's

MASSIVE CAJUN RESTAURANT WITH LARGE DANCE FLOOR; LIVE CAJUN MUSIC EVERY
NIGHT FROM 7 P.M. TO 10 P.M.

3480 Northeast
Evangeline Thwy. (I-49)
Lafayette, LA
70507
(337) 896-3247
prejeans.com/

There are times when Lafayette's fervent embrace of its Cajun heritage can be too much. Midway on a trip to Opelousas once, my party and I found ourselves famished and about to pass the service road exit for Prejean's on I-49. Prejean's is a massive restaurant, one that you might find yourself sitting outside of for an inordinate amount of time waiting for a table. My crew and I tried to occupy ourselves with small talk, a task made difficult with the gale-force Cajun music blasting from the PA. I looked around at the locals queuing up after us, collecting their little pagers, enduring this same blare as they milled about by the door. I wondered if they ever tire of Cajun music. I get that it's the heritage and a pretty rich one as heritages go, but if you are not out there dancing, those waltzes and two-steps can become a monotonous blur, one not improved with excessive amplification.

Like Grant Street, Prejean's opened in 1980, when it seems much of Lafayette was born in the midst of the oil boom that inflated the populations of a number of Louisiana towns. Bob Guilbeau had been working in California and was struck by how many Mexican restaurants featured live music and became cultural meeting places, and he sought to do the same on a patch of land he inherited from his grandparents. Prejean's boasts of being the "first Cajun-themed restaurant," a cautious distinction from Mulate's claim of being the original Cajun restaurant. Mulate's (in Breaux Bridge) also opened in 1980.

When the doors flew open and another fed family made it out to their truck, the blast of music was even louder. I wondered if it would just get louder and louder the farther you went in, eventually rattling your molecules loose like what happens at the rim of a black hole, when suddenly the music stopped and applause rippled through the place.

Lafayette

The band, without missing a beat, fell into another number just as our pager buzzed.

We got a table in the back, far enough from the music to nurse our rattled nerves with some top-notch Cajun cuisine. I will attest that Cajun restaurants that have live music are often not the ones with the best food, but Prejean's is an exception. Around the time Prejean's opened, Cajun food was being discovered worldwide, partially because of the popularity of chefs like New Orleans's Paul Prudhomme, who introduced a number of Cajun dishes into New Orleans's already famous Creole cuisine, and the homey nature of Cajun food was given an upgrade. Appetizers like fried green tomatoes smothered with crawfish in a sherry cream sauce or Prejean's signature catfish entrees, topped with lump crabmeat and grilled asparagus in a buttery wine sauce, are markedly dressier than the tried-and-true gumbos and étouffée simmering away around those Cajun tables when I grew up, yet they retain the threads of the culture. They enhance the greater Cajun theme, as it were.

Fully fortified for a night out in the depths of Opelousas, we made our way back into the mayhem of the dining room and crowded dance floor and passed the even larger crowd assembled outside the door, pagers in hand, and I saw how one could never get tired of this theme.

Zydeco Hall of Fame (formerly Richard's)
Teddy's Uptown Lounge

HALL OF FAME—CLASSIC, NO-FRILLS ZYDECO DANCE HALL; TEDDY'S—LAID-BACK "GROWN FOLKS" CLUB; BOTH WITH MUSIC ON A SPORADIC SCHEDULE

11151 Hwy. 190
Lawtell, LA
70570

When you ask anyone from years past where the zydeco bands used to play, they immediately say Richard's (pronounced *ree-shards*). It opened in 1947, the same year as Slim's Y-Ki-Ki, and over the years has hosted the likes of B.B. King and John Lee Hooker, as well as launching the careers of zydeco performers like John Delafose and Beau Jocque. The Richard family ran the club until 2006, when a family dispute led to it closing down. Michael DeClouet bought the building as well as the nightclub next door and rechristened it the Zydeco Hall of Fame after members of the Richard family would not relinquish the name.

It could not be a more unassuming building; were it not for the blinking sign out front and the line of cars parked out along the highway, it looks like a low-slung warehouse tucked away in the bend in the road, and even with the sign, I tend to pass it when I'm headed out to it. Walk in the front door and you are confronted with a picture of Amédé Ardoin flanked by a hand-painted sign that says BIG DOG. Ardoin, renowned for his virtuosity on the accordion and his distinctive high-pitched voice, appeared on one of the first recorded performances of the music of Acadiana back in 1929.

"NO PARKN ON THE DANCE FLOOR" is scrawled on the support beam that serves as an entry arch to that large room, which is flanked by crowded sections of small four-seater tables and chairs, decorated with hand-painted stars. Framed photographs of zydeco performers from over the years dot the wall behind them. Lil' Nathan, the headliner for the show that evening, has a song about wanting to appear on that very wall.

We arrived early to knock back canned beer from the bar

Lawtell

and take in the room. The gallery of portraits, zydeco stars of years past posing with their accordions, is lit by bare bulbs and beer signs, leaving the rest of the place in relative darkness. A single stage lines the back of the hall; the bar is cordoned off at the front. Otherwise, it is a large empty room.

After a crowd started to show up around nine, a DJ kicked into a set of contemporary R&B peppered with zydeco hybrids that couldn't be further from Ardoin's zydeco from the thirties, heavy on the bass and thick rhythms, even the presence of an AutoTune, a pitch-correcting voice modulator used in pop music lending a singer's voice a robotic tinge as it pulls it to the right note. The thrust of the song was that unmistakable zydeco shuffle beat, an integration of waltzes, two-steps, and blues cadences that became a thing of its own.

When asked what makes something zydeco, co-manager Rickey Richard explained, "It's that beat. You hear that beat and it's zydeco." I asked him what kind of chance for survival zydeco has, citing the frequent complaint among blues and Cajun musicians that their music and culture were dying out with the older players. "What the bands call zydeco now, it's not the traditional zydeco that we used to do. It's now a disco zydeco. They take an R&B song and make zydeco out of it, and the young people just follow it, and it's unbelievable." When asked why people come to this club that has been a zydeco mainstay for decades, only recently becoming the Zydeco Hall of Fame, he stated, "They come here to hear some zydeco. That's it."

The headliners that evening, Lil' Nathan and the Zydeco Big Timers, took the stage. Nathan's accordion kicked in, occasionally breaking into a loose, arpeggiated solo, but mostly slipped through that unstoppable beat like a vine. Many of the titles and lyrics of Lil' Nathan's songs, like much of contemporary zydeco, mention his or his band's name or his life spent playing this music; the word "zydeco" itself is often in the lyrics. The music and the artist and the club itself are in a perpetual state of self-assertion because they live this unlikely infectious music and because they adapt and roll with the times.

Lil' Nathan Williams Jr. is the scion of one of zydeco's dynasties—his father Nathan Williams Sr. fronts the legendary Zydeco Cha-Cha's, and his manager and uncle Sid Williams owns and operates the zydeco club El Sid O's in Lafayette. He grew up playing in his father's band and released his first CD when he was fourteen. Lil' Nathan went on to study jazz at the University of Louisiana, and that helped him broaden the often restrictive palette of zydeco. On albums, Lil' Nathan's accordion groove descends into the song to bolster up contemporary R&B vocals. The cover of *The Autonomous: Fit for Survival* finds him eschewing the cowboy getup for a slick white suit, posing with his accordion in front of a hotel swimming pool. He harmonizes about being snubbed by his girl at the mall on "Come Back to Me"; another song, "That L'Argent," features a remix with a rapper named Trucka. His MySpace page boasts, "My Wrath Has Just Begun & I Will Never Fail." Lil' Nathan is one of those artists Mr. Richard mentioned, changing the music with the times while retaining that beat that keeps it zydeco.

♫

Teddy's Uptown Lounge is directly across the gravel parking lot from the Hall of Fame. Unlike the utilitarian layout of the Hall of Fame, Teddy's is without confusion a nightclub. The black-and-white tiles on the sunken dance floor are laid out in concentric squares, as if they are forming a vortex under the single spinning disco light. Rickey Richard was laying down zydeco and soul from a laptop behind the bar, and Jeff Floyd's soul hit "Lock My Door" summoned the well-heeled regulars to the vortex.

The walls on one side are festooned with mirrors; on the other are tacked a dense array of snapshots from parties at the club along with flyers for dance lessons and other zydeco nights in the prairie region. Teddy's has live music occasionally or has soul and zydeco playing from a laptop through the sound system. I happened in there one night after Geno Delafose had celebrated his birthday at a concert in Eunice and the after-party spilled over into Teddy's. Geno's nephew Gerard Delafose and the Zydeco Gators were providing the entertainment.

At Teddy's, an older crowd holds court at the bar, dressed up for less-aerobic activity. A few couples get up and dance on the sunken checkered floor, reflected on the banks of mirrors lining the bar, but really, this is a place to be seen. I like to go back and forth between Teddy's and the Hall of Fame, especially since the Hall of Fame doesn't have air-conditioning and Teddy's has a fully stocked bar, but also because it grants a broader picture of the music and how it fits into the nightlife. It's true what my critic says, that it's about the dancers, but if you listen to the lyrics, the self-declarations of the songs, that sense of "being zydeco," how the names of the clubs find their way into the spaces between the accordion and yelps, how it can soundtrack a room full of sweaty bodies on the prowl as well as it does grown folks getting their drink on, you will find zydeco to be a reflection of the complex dynamic that defines the black Acadian community, its heritage and aspirations.

Mardi Gras Day in Mamou

Mamou is already not the easiest place to reach, planted out in the middle of the empty flatness of Evangeline Parish with little else around except a lot of rice, and on Mardi Gras, the one day of the year outsiders are called to its quaint streets, reaching it was proving to be impossible. U.S. 190, the once-major latitudinal artery through Louisiana before I-10 cut across the Atchafalaya, was roped off in Opelousas for its parades. No detour was offered, and the options to cut through town we got at the gas station at the eastern terminus of the parade route were a composite picture at best, the makings of great discourse but lousy directions. There was a moment of debate about just doing Mardi Gras in Opelousas, a place in which I have found it difficult to have an uninteresting time, but we had Mamou on our minds.

Each of us hazily remembered a great time we had had out there generally about ten years ago. My friend Annie remembered dancing with a guy with one leg. I remembered being surrounded by young gorgeous Cajun women at a street dance, each mean as a snake, and drunken boys staggering to keep from collapsing into a pile of gangly farmhand limbs. The dense mayhem of Fred's Lounge on Sixth Street was a blur. I could still distinctly remember the pork steak sandwich on white bread I bought from a guy with a grill. We huddled around our iPhone maps and veered into the network of empty roads webbing across Evangeline Parish hoping to find all this.

The bulk of my logistical experience in the prairie region of the state has involved half memories, conflicting info, and a slight amount of caginess. You get the feeling these communities lie off the grid for a reason, so that wandering fools like me won't come muddying up the tidy systems they have in place.

One's visitor status is persistently underscored by a friendly, if curious, "Y'all are not from around here." Which is fine; it is the *them* we seek out of Mamou to add flavor to our *us*.

As the roads wore on, and the less sure we were of each back road, frustration begged the question, whatever brought anyone out here in the first place? The obvious answer surrounded us in all directions: rice. This is the heart of Louisiana rice country, and like the endless acres of corn and soybeans that you drive through in the Midwest, the area around Mamou is given over to the yield of the land. One of the many stories about the name is that early Anglo-American settlers in the eighteenth century called the area "Mammoth Prairie" and the French who came after them shortened it to "Mamou." Our worries subsided when we passed the familiar pasture in Plaisance where the Zydeco Festival and trail ride take place and a humble green sign that pointed us to Mamou, where we met yet another thin rope at the north end of Sixth Street, barricading the town off from traffic.

There were horses being bridled among the scatter of BBQ pits in the Family Dollar parking lot, hip-hop blending with zydeco as you passed people tailgating from the back of cars, and a small tent stage proclaiming "'Big Mamou'—Heart of Cajun Country!" with a handful of couples making tight sidewinder zydeco circles straddling the double yellow line in the road. A folding table on the shoulder had elaborate cowboy hats for sale; another held a glaring array of silvery belt buckles. I wondered if this meant that Mamou had become more progressive over the years, for we all remembered the Mardi Gras street scene being a predominantly white affair. We consulted our maps again and found Fred's to be a mile to the south, so we decided to see how Mamou handled the transition between black celebrations and white and what lay in the middle.

As it turns out, not much. A strictly maintained divide between black and white Acadian cultures is common in the smaller towns of Acadiana. I've never really noticed any height-

Mardi Gras in Mamou

ened racial tension in these communities, but then perhaps this separation maintains it. It's unfortunate, given the similarities between the two cultures. A stray car revealed that we could have just made the block around the barricade and driven on to Fred's, parking as close as a block away; the paucity of traffic on our walk revealed that not many people made the trip.

On the southern end of the parade route there was another identical tent with a Cajun band reeling before a largely empty dance area. There was evidence of the horses having been through: Mamou starts its *courir*— a rampage of inebriated, costumed horsemen tearing across the countryside to collect chickens and shots of whiskey on the way—at Fred's, but it looked like the street action was largely over. I looked up from my phone to get a "y'all ain't from around here, are y'all?" look from a man walking by. When asked when things start kicking into gear, he said, "You are mostly looking at it." He claimed that over the years the festivities have dwindled in Mamou and that a lot of people in the area now go to Eunice. "Cultural changes." We shrugged and headed over to Fred's Lounge.

Fred's Lounge

THE QUINTESSENTIAL CAJUN BAR, ONLY OPEN SATURDAY MORNINGS AND MARDI GRAS DAY WITH TRADITIONAL CAJUN BANDS

420 Sixth St.
Mamou, LA
70554
(337) 468-5411

Fred's Lounge was packed to the gills in stark contrast to the scene outside on this Mardi Gras day in Mamou. The L around the bar was choked with revelers, nearly impassible, but some kind soul took a shine to the woman in our party and that gave us a conduit to the inebriation required to take in such a scene. The Lafayette Rhythm Devils were tearing away in a railed-off alcove to the back, decked out in their trademark prison stripes—they in fact looked incarcerated in their cordoned-off cell—as a cluster of dancers occupied the floor. It was Cajun done with just the right measure of drunk, keeping it loose but reverent.

People feel reverent about Fred's because it is one of those beloved places. A large historical plaque outside the door memorializes Alfred "Fred" Tate's purchase of the bar in 1946. In 1950, the lost art of the *courir* was revived in Mamou supposedly at one of the booths at Fred's, and in 1962 Revon Reed at KVPI 1050 AM in Ville Platte started remote-broadcasting a live Cajun music radio show there every Saturday morning, a tradition that continues today. In many people's eyes, Mamou is more a part of Fred's than the other way around.

While Fred's is especially packed during Mardi Gras, the scene is not all that different almost any Saturday morning, when the same radio station does a live simulcast of the Cajun Dance starting at 9 a.m. One morning in May, months after the collective hangover of Mardi Gras had passed and the fever of summer was just starting to come on, I found Jamie Berzas and Cajun Tradition in full swing. The bar was at about three-quarters the capacity of Mardi Gras day, which meant you had a little room to move, a little room to dance, a little room to drink—all the room you need in life.

Mamou

There were two distinct stars of the show that morning. The first was a guy everyone in the bar knew as Barry, wearing a red T-shirt stenciled with "Cajun Tradition," sitting in on triangle, or *t-fer*; the message it presented seemed more like a thesis statement than it did band merchandise, for there was something gravitational about the draw to this little bar. I overheard a few girls saying they'd come in from Houston, and the bikes lined up pointed to the bar being one stop on a poker run, but the crowd there that morning was distinctly Acadiana. When I needled up to the bar for a Bloody Mary, one old Cajun gal exclaimed, "Lord, it's been forever since I came out and did this!" When I asked how long forever was, "Oh let's see, it must have been four, maybe five weeks . . . maybe since Mardi Gras!"

Fred's serves as a counterbalance to the wide-open spaces of the Acadiana plains. You feel like you drive for miles with nothing in sight, and then suddenly you wind up in a place where everybody is. Barry clangs along with the band for a while, fetches the occasional drink for himself and his band mates, and makes the rounds flirting with women around the bar. It's not a bad gig to have.

I took a break from the Cajun mayhem and strolled down deserted Sixth Street, passing a barber shop with a Mayberryesque hand-painted sign on the plate glass, complete with a small depiction of Calvin peeing on Osama Bin Laden's head. The signage also stated that American Legion dues could be paid there, and the barber pole and the blue sky and holes in the awning reflected in the glass formed an implied American flag. Next door at a pawn shop, a rack of *courir* outfits—the wildly colored chicken suits the riders wear in the street parades on Mardi Gras day—hung near a glass vitrine displaying a pearly white, freshly pawned accordion. Among the LPs in a cardboard box in the back I found Freddy Fender's 1975 *Recorded Inside Louisiana State Prison* for a dollar.

Fortified by this respite, I forged back into Fred's just as Barry was sitting down to another set, and our second hero of the story made her appearance. Sue Tate, the widow of Fred

Jamie Berzas and Cajun Tradition performing at Fred's Lounge

Tate, is affectionately and universally known as Tante Sue. (*Tante* is Cajun French for "aunt.") She is the beloved feisty bartender and former owner of Fred's, and just as I found a vantage point to the side of the dance floor, she left her spot behind the bar to offer a cardboard box full of boudin to all takers, coquettishly hand-feeding a couple of pieces to the boys in the band. A few songs later, the band launched into the Cajun staple "Mardi Gras," and Tante Sue emerged from the back room with a fez and cape constructed from Crown Royal bags and led a snaking, lurching dance line through the bar, ratcheting up the wild scene to surreal levels.

Tante Sue took to the mic after a couple of swigs from the bottle of Hot Damn Schnapps holstered at her waist and addressed the crowd. "I have a few rules and regulations in here: I don't allow any kissin', and I have eyes behind my head. If you don't think I'll see you, I will. I don't allow any involvements of any form in here, I only allow beer or love," she offered at one point. "You heard me say beer first." She asked that we not bring in outside drinks and not try to dance with those procured from the bar in hand, but also added that we should not abandon those we love who are living in nursing homes. "If you do, the employees there will also."

Then she called for a waltz. Her voice has the weathered power of a field recording, somewhere between a haunting memory and an immediate holler, out of time and yet startlingly present. She intersperses her swaying and singing and swigs with hand motions, pointing an accusatory finger at the crowd, holding a palm up in momentary rapture, and even coyly playing air-accordion with the one printed on her T-shirt. Like Barry's red "Cajun Tradition" shirt, a Fred's T-shirt is more than merchandise—it's a statement of purpose.

To the uninitiated, or simply the underinebriated, Fred's Lounge can be a strong paradigm shift from one's usual Saturday morning, and you may find it difficult to slide back into the reality that waits right outside the door. Fortunately, a few steps farther will get you to the bar at the Hotel Cazan on the northwest corner of Sixth and Main.

Hotel Cazan

CLASSIC HOTEL BAR WITH LIVE MUSIC EARLY SATURDAY AFTERNOONS

401 Sixth St.
Mamou, LA
70554
(337) 468-5100
hotelcazan.com

J ust as the decor is a few notches more sophisticated at the Hotel Cazan than at Fred's Lounge, so is the musical experience. A few couples get up to dance, but mostly this is a listening place, and the bands accent the lyrical side of the music. The lilting drones of accordion and fiddles are often the only dancers in the room, echoes glancing off the marble floors and arcing midair. The music serves as a reminder of the breadth of Cajun culture, even in a postage-stamp–sized town like Mamou. Consider that back around the time the Cazan was built, there was a branch passenger line of the Southern Pacific running from Mamou to Eunice, one of the southernmost tendrils of the Rock Island line that brought passengers to and from the rest of the country. Hotels like this were showpieces for little railroad towns. The Cazan still is.

That particular Saturday morning, the drinks were commingling with history and the thought that no matter how off the grid one felt out here among the rice fields and the open sky, there was a larger social network laid over it, be it railroad or bikers on a poker run, and laid on top of that was something unique, something only this nexus could bring. Then, as if on cue to punctuate all these musings, here comes Barry from Fred's Lounge in his "Cajun Tradition" T-shirt, making the rounds at a couple of the tables until, t-fer in hand, he takes a seat with the band and commences to clang away.

Beau's Garage

CONTEMPORARY BAR-AND-GRILL IN CONVERTED GARAGE; VARIETY BANDS ON THE WEEKENDS

125 North Court St.
Opelousas, LA
70570
[337] 678-0648

Beau's Garage is a polished bar-and-grill ensconced in an old Conoco station that serves up the usual Cajun fare and features a small stage. It seems positively tony compared with Opelousas's other landmark haunts, and really I almost skipped it, but something about the band name Donnie & the Pooldoos pulled me in. A pulldoo, another name for the unassuming American coot, is not the most inspiring of Louisiana's wildlife; it's no bizarre pelican or stately egret. To honor such a creature by further misspelling it in the name of your bar band seems precisely the nod to middlebrow monoculture. With a band name this bad, I had to check them out. Plus, a beer and a catfish poboy after the long drive sounded pretty good too.

Donnie & the Pooldoos did as well. They are basically the classic rockabilly trio with lanky western men of unwavering talent and fieldhand humility augmented by the ubiquitous accordion, and while the small crowd seemed more into their poboys than they did the dance floor, the band did something a little amazing. Their set hinted at everything in their heritage: Hank Williams twang, Bob Wills swing, Ray Abshire grind. Their sound was as crisp and hot as the catfish I burned my mouth on at the bar. Nobody danced and the band didn't seem to mind. I'd love to hear these guys cut loose in a bar that would meet them halfway on the dance floor.

It was an important lesson for me, to not get too caught up in pinpointing the "authenticity" of a bar, a city, or a culture. Donnie & the Pooldoos and other bands that assimilate the culture into more popular frameworks are as much a part of the Louisiana nightlife heritage as the traditionalists that keep it real. Towns like Opelousas are treasures because somehow the traditional, the peculiar, manages to keep a foothold against the rising tide of American

Opelousas

cultural pasteurization—but it is important to remember that
they are real towns in the here and now, ones that keep moving
according to their own plan.

Slim's Y-Ki-Hi

MASSIVE ZYDECO CLUB WITH LIVE ZYDECO BANDS ON SPORADIC WEEKENDS

8410 Hwy. 182
(North Main St.)
Opelousas, LA
70570
(337) 942-6242
slimsykiki.com/

I usually find myself coming to Opelousas by plunging out of the dark. The town erupts from the crossroads of Highway 190, the old road, and I-49, the new, a little like Brigadoon, mysterious out there in the flat and the fog. I'm romanticizing a city that by most assessments is not all that romantic; the highway splits as it crosses the city, passing the usual glut of convenience stores and fast-food places threatening to choke out the vestiges of the sweet downtown and the cozy little trailer park, and when you reach the terminus at either end, the road snaps back and you are in the dark again. It is only in veering off that main road that the city's peculiar yet equally phantasmal treasures can be found.

Jump off the main road to the north, back into darkness, and you will find the beating heart of zydeco, a music and lifestyle that are a product of curious influences. Zydeco, at least the version of it practiced in Opelousas, is a Creole product. In the general sense, the word "creole" means a group of disparate cultures finding a means by which their identifying hallmarks can mix. In the Opelousas zydeco sense, Creole is manifested by African American men in cowboy clothes playing Cajun-influenced R&B on accordions.

Slim's Y-Ki-Ki is not the easiest place to find even once you acclimate yourself to Opelousas's nest of one-way streets—coming from the east on 190, take a right at Checker's on Union Street, follow it until it joins up with Main Street, bear to the right at Martin Luther King Jr. Drive, and keep going about a quarter mile. There is no mistaking it when you get there; a bright yellow sign with music notes and the boast "The Original Zydeco Club" (it opened in 1947) will guide you in. On Fridays or Saturdays when there's a show, the parking lot is usually filled to capacity at 10 p.m.,

Moving to the music at
Slim's Y-Ki-Ki

and you will have to find a spot on
the narrow neighborhood street to
park.

Walking into Slim's is like a
cinematic dream sequence, disori-
enting but compelling. It's a huge
place but with a low ceiling and
even lower lights. Scattered tables
haphazardly line the perimeter of
the club as if the room had been
hastily cleared for the dance. The
only lights besides those for the stage are from the bar to one
side and the occasional beer sign. Otherwise, the room is an expanse of shadows and silhouettes moving in herky-jerky circles
to the music.

I say "stage," but in actuality, Slim's has two stages positioned
on the back and left sides of the dance floor, so that as one band
finishes, the second band can jump right in, and the assembled
crowd merely needs to pivot in their small circles on the shadowy dance floor. It is a markedly efficient way to do things.

On the particular night I first went to Slim's, after receiving
a speeding ticket in Krotz Springs—the speed limit drops suddenly to 45 when you cross the overpass, and the cops on the
west side of the bridge are well acclimated to the dark—JoJo
Reed and the Happy Hill Zydeco Band were at the left stage,
warming up the crowd gathering for Keith Frank and the Soileau Zydeco Band.

Keith Frank and band stood resolute on the still-darkened
main stage of Slim's, like silhouetted superheroes waiting for
the moment to act. They kicked in just as Reed and crew hit
their last lick, and like a tick of the greater clockwork of zydeco,
the near-capacity crowd made a quarter turn on their heels to
face him. One yelp, and the entire place—band, music, crowd,
and all—went into overdrive. The darkened dance floor was
more densely populated as you approached the center; on the
periphery, there were a couple of older men showing off their

moves among others standing around, but as you got deeper in, it was a thicket of hands in the air and feet doing a complicated strutting dance. This density, the pulling from sources that pull from other sources, and the swirling intensity of the music all point back to the reality of zydeco. Zydeco is synergy music, taking the overlap of racial and musical influences, the pile-up of tradition and innovation, and forming a vortex powered by the incessant beat and accordion, capable of sucking everything into it.

The same person who attempted to dissuade me from my "wonky music critic" ways in Breaux Bridge one morning at Café Des Amis pointed out that my impression of zydeco clubs was also way off base, that these places were not about the music but the dancers, and I think she's half right. Cajun music and zydeco are not spectator sports, and the real energy of both play out on the dance floor, but I contend that there is something more primal at play in these darkened dance halls than just showing off your steps.

Zydeco brings out the libidinous side of its dancers. The couples out in the dim center of the floor were less dancing with each other than at each other, dance steps becoming a twisting back and forth on a spot on the floor accompanying the room-shaking beat and a barrage of grunts and yelps. It can be like watching cobras square off. It bears noticing that while couples grind away in the center of the room, there is often a ring of men around the perimeter decked out in fine zydeco plumage: cowboy hat, a giant belt buckle, western shirt and boots. Occasionally you see an outfit that verges on costume: hat, belt, and jacket bedazzled with studs worn by a wolf-hungry man looking for an opening, a woman alone in the throng of sidewinding feints and darts. The tension rises as the dance floor fills up, like any concentration of particles in motion.

The Rainbow Inn

**RUSTIC SWAMP BAR; OPEN WEDNESDAY AND THURSDAY EVENINGS; SWAMP POP STAR
DON RICH PLAYS REGULARLY ON WEDNESDAYS**

La. Hwy. 70 South
Pierre Part, LA
70339
(985) 252-8069

On our way out to the Rainbow Inn in the relatively isolated swamp community of Pierre Part, my buddy Clarke and I got lost. We'd turned down what we thought was La. 69 but instead found ourselves on a gravel road plunging into a sugarcane field, a fallen tree cut in half lying on either side. I don't usually get out to such off-the-path places as these, or, more correctly, I don't get out of the car when I do, but the lure of seeing the stars without the light pollution of civilization was calling. The heavens cast before me in the cold night air were spellbinding until it occurred to me that some other lost soul might barrel right into us as we had to this spot, so we left the stars behind in favor of our planned destination.

We were blaring a Valcour sampler, *Allons Boire un Coup: A Collection of Cajun and Creole Drinking Songs,* particularly to hear my friend Dickie Landry (swamp pop legend and, curiously, a founding member of the Philip Glass Ensemble) lay down a thermonuclear sax solo over a Chris Stafford fuzzed-out arrangement of the staple "Parlez-Nous à Boire." It's a defiantly cool version of a song we've heard a million times, one that speaks to the raucous history of rowdy backwoods bars. It spurs a lot of "Now *this* is how it should be done" remarks, for we are self-appointed experts in how it should be done, apparently. It keeps us in good company through the stretch of La. 70 and until we hit the overflowing parking lot of the Rainbow Inn.

The Rainbow Inn is famous for its persistence, perched since the 1930s upon the thin strip of land between the bayous that form Pierre Part. When we arrived, the clear night reflecting on the nexus of waters crisscrossing the road and the ambient bob of fishing boats tied up nearby

and the quiet rush of cars created a spellbinding scene—and there again were those stars hidden away from us city folk. Had it not been so cold on this Thursday night in December, we would have lingered a little longer, but fortunately, stars of a different sort awaited us inside.

Don Rich, Pierre Part's most renowned contribution to the swamp pop pantheon, was holding court on the bar's ample stage, and men in camouflage jackets swung gals in tight-fitting jeans, teetering on high-heeled boots, around the dance floor. Don has a handle on seven different instruments from sax to fiddle to accordion, but tonight he's manning the band from behind the keyboards. He started playing music in his teens some thirty-two years ago in this very club, or so says Miss Cora, the bar's owner.

Miss Cora spied me taking notes at the far end of the bar and sidled over to investigate. She's got three generations of her family manning the bar with her. "They saw you writing stuff down, so I figured I'd better come check. The ABC board's been in here enough times that I knew you weren't them." Cora opens the bar generally every Wednesday and Thursday night, "and maybe Friday if I'm still thirsty," she jokes.

"Don's been playing for me since he was fourteen, started him at $10 a night. His first paying gig and he's still playing here." I point out to Clarke the gray T-shirt of a woman standing nearby, the back of which was emblazoned with a picture of Don and his massively toothy smile, circled by the simple declarative, "I'm a Don Rich fan." Clarke offered, "Thing is, I think I am too now."

I nodded in agreement. Don Rich's recorded output has largely been too polished, too saccharine for my feral tastes, but live, here in his home bar, he is a soul machine. Swamp pop as it is currently practiced is often burdened with too much reverence, the strength in the material lying more in the memories of it than in the continuation of it, and yet I'm always surprised at the number of young fans it draws. On this night, the ratio of younger folks near the bar and the pool table to the older crowd stationed at tables off to the side is two-to-one. Everyone is into it, though; the youngest bartender mouths the words of the song as she gets drinks, and Don shouts, "À boire!" to folks he's undoubtedly known his whole life.

The real reason they are into it, though, is the life Rich breathes into these old songs, R&B standards that have had the soul Michael McDonald-ed and Michael Bolton-ed out of them over the years. I half expect all the remaining loose paint on the bar's peeling beadboard roof to come cascading off in a torrent as he tears through an Otis Redding tune or the late Bobby Charles's "Tennessee Blues," as well as his own "Every Day Can Be Like a Holiday." His band is great, giving each tune a muscular swing worthy of any backwater beer joint, but the secret weapon is his trumpet player, a crystal blare cutting through the soft edges of the sax and the blur of keyboards. It doesn't steal the show, but it punctuates it. Swamp pop bands should give the trumpet player more stage time.

It's a magic night under the stars in otherwise picture-still Pierre Part, one that only gets a little brighter when Miss Cora's daughter gestures to some of the young men in camo jackets. "A couple of those guys from *Swamp People* are in here tonight. They filmed in here a couple of times. Last time mama got a speaking part as well." *Swamp People,* if you don't know, is a reality show on the History Channel following a number of families of alligator hunters as they ply their trade in the surrounding swamps. It's the kind of show that sensationalizes these little-known pockets of life without turning them into a circus, sort of how Don Rich rocks these old songs like they are brand new.

Bourque's Social Club

RUSTIC BLUES AND FOLK CLUB WITH SPORADIC SCHEDULE; BYOB

1012 St. Mary Ave.
Scott, LA
70583
myspace.com/
bourquessocialclub

On the western outskirt of Lafayette lies the little town of Scott, a sleepy exit like many on I-10 that you might never think to take, one that leads to a modest neighborhood perched around a set of train tracks, yet along those tracks in this neighborhood is one of the coolest music venues around, not for what it has but for what it doesn't have. It doesn't have food, it doesn't sell beer, and it doesn't have flat-screen TVs, or even air-conditioning. All it has is music and a room off the beaten path where it gets played. Bourque's Social Club is the real stuff.

In 1902 Albert Bourque started his social club in the building on St. Mary Avenue as a place where culture can be experienced in the little town fifteen miles west of Lafayette. Blues musician and, since the 2010 BP oil spill, political activist Drew Landry runs the place now, much in the same spirit as Mr. Bourque. The shows take place roughly twice a month and eschew the orthodoxy that often limits a blues or folk club. Recent acts appearing at the club include country gospel legend Charlie Louvin, indie rock/outré Americana artist Viking Moses, and, on one magic night, Excello recording artist Lazy Lester, along with Rudy Richard and Lil' Buck Senegal on guitar, underappreciated R&B singing legend Carol Fran, and Excello session drummer Clarence "Jockey" Etienne on drums.

I keep mentioning Excello because that label is key to the development of Louisiana blues, injecting the early singles by Slim Harpo, Lightnin' Slim, and Lazy Lester into the DNA of popular music. Lester found his way into this cadre one afternoon in the mid fifties when he recognized Lightnin' Slim riding the same bus. He passed his stop and followed Slim to Jay Miller's studio in Crowley. The harmonica player for the session was a no-show, and the producer tapped Lester to fill in.

Scott

Lester recorded his first Excello single, "I'm Gonna Leave You Baby/Lester's Stomp," in 1956, gaining notoriety for his slurred delivery and wild country side, which has never abated over the years.

In contrast to the smooth uptown version of the blues that we experience a lot in these parts, Lazy Lester seems downright wild, stomping out rhythms on the hardwood floor, blowing his harp like a train whistle. It is telling that the New Orleans swamp roots bonanza the Ponderosa Stomp took its name from one of Lester's song titles. Rudy Richard, sitting in on guitar for the main set, told me before the show, "A lot of people think Lester is a little cuckoo because of how he comes across, but let me tell you, he's got it down tight."

This was readily apparent as he led the all-star band through classics like "Blood Stains on the Wall" by Honeyboy Pat and Lester's signature tune, "They Call Me Lazy," cracking jokes between the numbers, throwing out non sequiturs like "I'm not as good as I once was but I'm once as good as I ever was" or "That means 'Get in there and wash them dishes before that water gets cold'" in response to a short delay after one song.

Bourque's is the kind of place where you want to see a show like this. The perimeter of the high-ceilinged, white-washed room was packed with music lovers there to listen, yet there was no sense of overt reverence to the place. A number of them propped their feet up on ice chests they brought with them— Bourque's is BYOB—just happy to be there in the company of these personalities. Others chatted about Excello history around the merchandise table set up in the back. This felt like "the real stuff" that blues aficionados peruse.

The truth is, the real stuff was already long dormant when college kids in the sixties started latching onto old Folkways records looking for some kind of authenticity with which to combat the staid normalcy of the fifties. Many of the blues artists we consider to be the classics were long forgotten and resurrected to fill this market. Lester was not one of these artists. By the time the folk revival came around, Lester had long given up on the music industry and had moved up to Michigan with Slim Harpo's sister to fish and eke out a living doing odd jobs. In the ensuing years, his songs were covered by the Kinks, the Fabulous Thunderbirds, and most notably Freddy Fender, who had a 1977 hit with Lester's 1958 b-side "Sugar-Coated Love."

Lester took to the stage again after the crowd had thinned, this time with just an acoustic guitar, and worked through a short set of mostly Hank Williams tunes. If you thought "Wedding Bells" is heart-wrenching when Hank does it, you are unprepared for the gravitas Lester gave it. It came out of him raspy and forlorn, a ghost of a song haunting the room. This is where the real stuff happened for me. We were no longer in the presence of a blues legend running through his own beloved songs or crowd favorites; we were witnessing the eternal anguish and love that threads through all we human beings have to express. The lines between country and blues, now and then, history and revision all faded in that fateful moan like I suspected it has in that room for more than a century. It reminded you that the real stuff is elusive, impossible to pinpoint. You just have to be glad to be in the neighborhood.

Jean Lafitte National Park's Wetlands Acadian Cultural Center

MUSEUM WITH AUDITORIUM; TRADITIONAL CAJUN MUSIC JAM ON MONDAY EVENINGS

314 St. Mary St.
Thibodaux, LA
70301
(985) 448-1375
nps.gov/jela/wetlands-
acadian-cultural-
center.htm

When we talk about local culture, what do we really mean? Do we mean preserving that which grew from our native soil as opposed to that which was imported? Are we obliged to become fans of that indigenous culture, even when it is something that, left to our own devices, we'd pass by? Those are the thoughts that occupied my mind one Monday afternoon when I jumped in my car directly after six hours of teaching to drive the hour and a half to Thibodaux to take in the Cajun music sessions at Jean Lafitte National Park's Wetlands Acadian Cultural Center. I love Cajun music probably more than I like it, in that what it represents—the rarely seen human instinct to not let something be destroyed over time—is inspiring to me. I love the community spirit of it, the way old people get out to dance, the sprinkling of young people who keep its flame fueled. I've said it before: we have something really special here in Cajun culture, and frankly, it is remarkable that it has survived as well as it has.

The Wetlands Acadian Culture Center is a well-appointed brick building on Highway 1, right in the middle of Thibodaux, containing a public library, museum, and performance hall. A historical marker out front claims that it sits at the "Confluence of Bayous," a rather melodious term for the junction of Bayous Lafourche and Terrebonne. The Acadians came in 1785, and the village of Thibodaux was founded on the banks of this confluence a few years later.

The informal concert was under way when I entered the theater. Eight musicians were on stage, and about triple that number of people were in the audience, unfortunately underscoring the waning public interest in the

music. The group was not a tight dance-floor-seasoned outfit but rather a group of nonprofessionals who had an interest in keeping the informal, back-porch jam side of Cajun music alive. The park ranger Bill Finney shared with the group that his French teacher had helped him out with some lyrics and he was going to attempt singing in French, and there they went. The performers were as follows: Roland Landry on harmonica, Finney and Camille LeBoeuf on acoustic guitar, Larry LeBoeuf on the most gorgeous '64 Fender Jaguar I have had the pleasure of seeing and hearing ("I bought it new when I was nineteen and am still playing it today at sixty-three," said LeBoeuf), Willy Champagne on acoustic guitar, Francis Foret on fiddle, Norman Landry on accordion and rhythm guitar (he also sang in French and English), and Agnes Landry keeping the boys in line on the *t-fer* or "little iron," less exotically known as the triangle.

What came out of this group was not the well-oiled machine that you get in a Breaux Bridge dance hall. Instead it was contemplative in nature. These lovesick waltzes issued into the air like smoke from a flame that burned hotter decades ago. The ambiance was sweet and informal; at one point Finney asked if there were any out-of-towners in the audience, and a group from Virginia and a couple from Pennsylvania introduced themselves, and the performers chatted with them from the stage during the song breaks. It was about as friendly a concert as one could attend; one couple even got up and danced across the stage during one number, but the show made me a little sad; you could feel that this kind of performance was not going to be around much longer.

Then they kicked into "Evangeline" and it all abruptly pivoted. Larry and his Jaguar gave the tune a haunting, almost Hawaiian undertone, while two harmonicas slowly weaved in a dreamy hum to the accordion lines. It gave this tune I've heard a million times a celestial quality, without taking anything away from the traditions from which it came. I was shocked at how beautiful this tune could become when people brought their own experiences to it. It reminded me that culture is a living thing; if it stagnates, it dies, and Cajun life, like everything else in the universe, is perpetually evolving. It will never be like it used to be, but thanks to folks like these, it can grow into something just as special.

NEW ORLEANS and ENVIRONS

The Green Room

CASUAL DOWNTOWN BAR THAT CATERS TO THE NORTHSHORE'S BOHEMIAN STRAIN

521 East Boston St.
Covington, LA
70433
greenroomlive.net/

When I set out for clubs on the fringes of south Louisiana—on any trip for that matter—I often put more thought into my playlist than things like fuel and directions. The iPod is a lifesaver for playlist lunatics like myself—now it's just a matter of loading up this little blob of plastic and design savvy rather than spending my evening careening down a dark highway, trying to fetch the pile of jewel cases slipping under my feet. These trips give me a rare hour or so where I may suckle at my current obsession, and this time it was the 13th Floor Elevators, the Texan group led by future rock-madness poster boy Roky Erikson, who in 1966 perfected the art of psychedelic rock. His feral scream, the weird reverbed bongos in the background, the unstoppable propulsive energy in those loose recordings made the trip worth taking, regardless of destination.

This Wednesday evening's mission was to head for the Green Room in Covington to take in its acoustic night—hoping for the best, prepared for the worst. Acoustic nights can be a real crapshoot—you might get a singer-songwriter with a flayed-open soul, or you might get a dour college student who just discovered Bob Dylan, wearing a shiny new harmonica holder bought off the Web. I love acoustic music, not because I think the performer is that much closer to the bone than when plugged in, but because an acoustic guitar somehow forces performers to dig in and show more of themselves. Those six strings are like a slingshot in a way, pushing you out into the air with each pluck, and you want to see where you are going.

As I pulled into downtown Covington (Roky and the boys intoning "the kingdom of heaven is within you" with delicious, sensuous menace), I was pleasantly

Covington

stunned at how cool the town seemed. I guess my Covington experiences in the past had consisted mostly of getting gas right off the interstate. But here I was across from Edie, a bustling upscale restaurant with what looked like some adventurous design; large, loud paintings beaming through the window at the St. Tammany Arts Association; a bustling coffee shop on the corner; people out and about at 9 o'clock on a Wednesday night. I'm down with this kind of scene.

The Green Room has a nondescript entrance on Boston Street, right next to the much more flamboyant, kitschy Buster's Place (formerly Vic 'n' Nat'Ly's Restaurant). But once I pushed past the door (with the Elevators in my earbuds pointedly proclaiming, "Before you accuse me, you better look at yourself"), I was suddenly ensconced in the student apartment of my dreams. The place is one large room with couches along the walls, tables haphazardly populating the floor, guitars and amps in islands around the room, and candles everywhere. The bar was nicely tucked away to the back, leaving room up front for the stage.

As the DJ went through a subdued mix of low-key dance and indie rock, I spied the bongo set sitting on a chair on the stage. If you see bongos at an acoustic jam, it's generally a good sign in my book. Mark St. James, the Green Room's booking manager, dropped by the couch (can I say I wish every club allowed me the privilege of watching a show from a couch in the back?) to give me the lowdown.

"On acoustic nights (every Wednesday) people come out of the woodwork, some with set material, some who just get up and jam," he said. "We are more of a music club than a bar, really. It's a place for music lovers with a really casual vibe. People here would have to go down to New Orleans for that until we opened up."

He drifted off to adjust the lights for The Enablers, an acoustic guitar and bass duo led by Blake Selmon. The Enablers played a rich set with remarkable variety for an acoustic group, working from George Jones's "He Stopped Loving Her Today" to Led Zeppelin's "California" to Nirvana's "All Apologies," Selmon giving each its due while adding his own particular bent. Acoustic acts are unfortunately often exercises in over-reverence, so this was perfect. The drummer for the following act, dubbed "The Project," joined in on most of the songs, giving them a little more meat without swallowing the guitars whole.

After The Enablers finished, the stage started to fill up with multiple guitarists, two drummers, and a couple of guys pouring over college-rule notebooks. Elise Wheeler, a regular at the club and friend of one of the performers, explained that this was a funk, rock, blues jam—with her friend doing spoken word over it. While they prepared for liftoff, I asked her why she comes to the Green Room. "The people, the atmosphere—there is nowhere around here with good live music this consistently."

Around then, The Project kicked in with an infectious barrage of lysergic funk rock, reminiscent of the early Funkadelic records where they grafted acid rock onto soul and birthed a glorious monster. Nick Hasslock was the spoken-word artist here, delivering a chantlike flow of socially conscious poetry that darted in and out of the infinite groove the band was shooting for. I am, generally, not a fan of "jam band" music because it usually starts nowhere and goes nowhere without incident, but The Project felt alive and dangerous—exquisite stuff. They played two extended pieces, but in psychedelic terms, that stretched to nearly an hour. Elise and Mark were both right about the vibe here; it bounced off every surface and through every person. I reluctantly packed up my stuff for the drive home, with the Elevators' sole hit, "You're Gonna Miss Me," blasting in my ears.

The Howlin' Wolf Northshore

CONTEMPORARY NIGHTCLUB WITH ROOTS, CAJUN, AND VARIETY BANDS

1623 Montgomery St.
Mandeville, LA
70448
(985) 626-1616
thehowlinwolf.com/

The lakefront area of Old Mandeville, bordered by Highway 190, the causeway, the lake, and Fontainebleau State Park, is unabashedly charming. As I tooled around the narrow streets on a lazy Sunday, I spied plenty of little homespun restaurants and boutiques. I spent some time on the walking path snaking the shoreline of the shockingly vast Lake Pontchartrain. I passed a gaggle of ladies all in purple congregated at the steps of the venerated Rip's Restaurant, their chatter a counterpoint to the click of pool balls at Don's a couple of doors down, all underscored by the languid swish of the lake. It was both laid back and active, about as close to the languor of a beach town as you will get in Louisiana.

On this visit I had hoped to catch the Cajun fais-do-do that takes place every Sunday at the new Northshore branch of the Howlin' Wolf, one of the most venerated New Orleans live-concert settings, but at the last minute I caught an announcement saying it was canceled that week. I opted for a show I would never attend of my own volition: Frontiers—A Tribute to Journey. In a lot of live-music towns, tribute bands are seen as a cultural death knell, but the more I thought about it, a Journey tribute band sounded perfect.

The Howlin' Wolf was smart to set up shop here in Old Mandeville. At its various Warehouse District locations, the Howlin' Wolf serves to reflect a different New Orleans—not just the brass bands and New Orleans funk but its singer-songwriter side, its roots rock community, a more homey side of the city—and this fits in perfectly with the laid-back atmosphere of the Northshore.

I got turned around in the dark that had descended by the time I reached the end of the bridge, but by the grace of iPhone's GPS and map-

Mandeville

ping capabilities, I landed, starving, at the doorstep of Juniper Restaurant for a preconcert meal. The tasso-encrusted fish and tangy Boston Blue salad set me right and prepared for whatever the night held in store.

I trusted my phone to once again take me through the dark streets of Old Mandeville, and for a moment, I thought I had plugged in the wrong address for the Howlin' Wolf. But when I caught a trio of women in summer finery headed toward a block with cars pulled over in the grass, I figured I was in the right place. They had quite a crowd for Journey, or the approximation thereof, and I had to park about two blocks away. In the dark passing the Mandeville Cemetery, surrounded by a chorus of frogs and a blanket of stars I'm not accustomed to seeing on my way to a bar, I saw the club aglow in a clearing, as if it had grown unexpectedly in the woods.

The building is somewhere between a barn and a church, high-ceilinged and spacious with a loft balcony that rings the inside. The modest stage takes up one end of the room with the bar to one side and a lounge area with couches on the other. A large wooden deck surrounds the place for those moments of escape, where waitresses circulate, filling drink orders. The crowd was older, congenial, and ready to relive their (and my) golden years through the simulacrum of Frontiers. I was trying to maintain my cool distance, but I kept thinking what a great bar it was. Fully air-conditioned, not too loud, no pretention, no hassle.

Frontiers took the stage, and I spent the first few songs sending smart-ass texts like "I hope that on a rough day at the dealership, Not Steve Perry points to the sky and hits that one note that makes it all better" to my friends, but the undeniable charm of Journey wore down my defenses. The crowd and band hit a synergistic point with "Faithfully," everyone, including myself, swaying with the "whoa-oh-oh-oh's" at the end as Not Steve Perry soared high above us. Sure, it was maybe not the most culturally indigenous musical moment in my experience, but like Mandeville itself, it put a sincere smile on my face.

Ruby's Roadhouse

CLASSIC ROADHOUSE BAR WITH LIVE ROOTS, SOUL, AND ROCK ON A SPORADIC SCHEDULE

840 Lamarque St.
Mandeville, LA
70448
(985) 626-9748
rubysroadhouse.com/

The venerable Ruby's Roadhouse has been open in the same spot for ninety years, a gathering place for bikers and retirees, regional blues bands, and tourists in search of authenticity. *Car and Driver* dubbed it one of the ten best roadhouse bars in the country. Regional blues acts pack the house on Saturday nights; even actor and self-styled bluesman Steven Seagal played there once, but we'll get to that in a minute. On the balmy Sunday night I visited, the warm glow of the half-empty honky-tonk revealed a homier scene.

The first thing I saw was a cackling woman crouched on the floor, petting a dog belonging to one of the patrons. Van Halen's "Runnin' with the Devil" was playing overhead, accompanied by a character at the bar who, despite some trouble with the lyrics and general singing technique, embodied the spirit of the song. I'd found what I was looking for and ordered a beer.

The patrons of Ruby's are a lot like any great family—sure, maybe a little dysfunctional, but there is a marked strain of love in their interactions. The bartender offered up the "Ruby's Diary," a heavy guestbook filled with page-long ruminations of good times past. On the opening page is a telling inscription: "HAVE YOU FOUND ANY FALSE TEETH BY THE POOL TABLE, TIM?"

As you progress through the book, the pages get more ornate, and sketches and doodles appear among the testaments. One page was drawn up like a formal certificate with a banner emblazoned "NOTICE OF TERMINATION," where a former employee thoughtfully laid out his failings including the cryptic "failure to meet the company's chin hardware requirement." He even had blanks for witnesses to sign it. I've seen people get fired from a bar before, but never with such amiability. I flipped through looking for

Mandeville

some Zen inscription from Steven Seagal and couldn't find one, but when I asked about that night when the action star dropped by, I was directed to something much better—Nicole.

Nicole has been a regular at Ruby's for years, longer than she and her husband, Tim, could pinpoint. She was the 2005 queen of the Ruby's Mardi Gras Parade that starts at Don's by the lake and ends in the Ruby's parking lot. She is the owner of Mojo, the dog sitting at the foot of her bar stool, and runs the local Merle Norman. She was there the night Seagal played.

"He shows up with [former New Orleans police chief] Eddie Compass and some state troopers as his personal bodyguards. He's been at a party on the back patio and the crowd parts like the Red Sea and he taps me on the shoulder asking if he can have our table." Nicole points to the table where she and her friends like to play dice. "I asked him if he wanted to play dice, but he had this *funga* face, all serious and I'm like, 'Hell no, you can't have my table!' He wandered around for a while and then got up and played guitar for thirty minutes or so. He was no Tab Benoit, but he was all right. We had our buzz on so we weren't star struck."

I got the feeling Nicole and this bar have a million stories: "There was the time a biker accidentally shot himself in the thigh right here, between me and my cousin Monique." Down near the base of the bar was the bullet hole. "Also I met Melissa Gilbert at one of the benches over there by the wall. She was really nice." The bartender cut in to tell me about the ghost that inhabits the building. "He makes the sound of pool balls breaking when you first unlock the door." I had the feeling the stories would continue to unfold as long as I stood there, but I got what I came for. I finished my beer, petted Mojo on the head, and wandered out, confident that there will be more stories on my next visit.

Checkpoint Charlie's

GRUNGY BAR WITH LOCAL ROCK, PUNK, AND ROOTS MUSIC

501 Esplanade Ave.
New Orleans, LA
70116
(504) 281-4847
myspace.com/
checkpoints

Checkpoint Charlie's lies like an outpost, a lookout on the edge of the French Quarter's residential district. It's a bit of a dump actually, one of those New Orleans bars that make you wonder if they ever finished the place or if it just eroded to this state over the years. Like any good outpost, it covers all your basic needs, in this case: no cover, cheap beer, greasy food, live music, and, should things get messy, a Laundromat. Add to that a colorful clientele.

One evening at Checkpoint Charlie's, about a year after Katrina, I caught The Zydepunks, a riotous quintet of fiddle, bass, drums, and two accordionists, tearing through their set of swampy punk waltzes and tangos before a mixed crowd of mohawked punk revivalists, drunks, and college kids, reeling with carefree abandon. Despite the Cajun association with the accordions and the zydeco reference in their name, the Zydepunks are neither and instead reflect the wide scope of New Orleans musical influences, injecting their gypsy punk with French, Irish, and Baltic. They are a drunken revelry laced with outrage. Juan Kuffner of the Zydepunks explains about his lyrics, "They present a bleak, dreary, angry vision of how things are in New Orleans and Louisiana right now, with the occasional glimmer of hope."

It's difficult to say whether, in the years since then, New Orleans's outlook has gotten any brighter. It is almost like the place laughed off the sobriquet "The City That Care Forgot" until it came true. You'd never know anything of significance happened as you navigate the perpetual drunks on Bourbon Street. The bars and strip joints on Bourbon seem focused more on the quantity than the quality of the New Orleans thing. Here folks are trying to pack in as

New Orleans

much of their concept of New Orleans as possible before the alcohol poisoning takes hold. It's why I think local dives like Checkpoint Charlie's are so key to understanding New Orleans, a city more ramshackle and glorious than any tourist brochure or tourist bar can convey.

Circle Bar

FUNKY BAR AND INTIMATE LIVE LOCAL MUSIC VENUE IN AN OLD MANSION; OPEN WEEKDAYS 4 P.M. TO 4 A.M., WEEKENDS 9 A.M. TO 4 A.M.; MUSIC MOST NIGHTS

1032 St. Charles Ave.
New Orleans, LA
70130
(504) 588-2616
myspace.com/
thecirclebar

If I had to handpick a bar to stand in for the infamous House of the Rising Sun, it might be Circle Bar. A haunted mansion of a place on Lee Circle that plays ramshackle host to much of the city's underground music scene, the Circle Bar is a quintessential New Orleans club. It's an old house that has seen minimal renovation in its transformation to a nightclub: an elongated bar stretches down the length of what might have been a dining room, and the artists play huddled in a parlor shooting off to one side. Suspended from the roof, staring down at you like you're in Alice's Wonderland, is a giant clock from the old K&B Drug Store chain. You can probably pack about forty people in there. I've seen everything from a Monkees tribute band to blistering garage punk to avant-garde ensembles creating a homespun sine wave vibration with stringed instruments, guitars, and effects. It all makes sense in such a nonsensible setting.

New

Frenchmen Street, New Orleans

Saying New Orleans is a city built up of nightclubs is like saying matter is built up of molecules, a true if reductionist statement. Nearly everyone in the world has some concept of New Orleans that revolves around some concept of those bars. Having spent the majority of my life in a low orbit around these places, I think of them as a series of open doorways each with their own shade of dim light emanating from within, a multifaceted possibility when I started going to New Orleans as a teenager, a potentially serious issue as a college student, and now a distinct way of living. Drunks and the crumbling houses they inhabit don't exactly offer the strongest foundation for a city, but they do give New Orleans its lean.

A night out in New Orleans telescopes from dinner or coffee to some music, to another bar, and then to another, and then to someone's house for a party in some part of the city you've never even seen before, to eventually a hangover, to, if there is any kindness in your schedule the next day, a late lunch. In most of the pieces for this book, I've tried to formulate a general theory of a town by its houses of leisure, but that is a complicated, tangled task in New Orleans, and the best I can offer is a couple of threads to follow.

On this particular outing I skipped Bourbon Street and headed instead toward Frenchmen Street, which runs along the back side of the French Quarter in a neighborhood called the Marigny. I found a parking spot somewhere deep in the Marigny's grid, wandering a little lost among the picturesque shuttered homes in the residential section downriver from the Quarter. Then I saw a guy careen by on a double-decker bicycle, two bikes welded comically together like a Dr. Seuss invention, so I knew I was close.

The section of Frenchmen Street between Washington Park and its terminus at Esplanade is where the indigenous and tourist areas of a complicated city like New Orleans overlap. It's a place where those busy defining an identity come to be seen and others come to see them and soak up their aura. It can be a curtain between the two sides of New Orleans, or perhaps a fault where tectonic plates collide and buckle. I started this night at Frenchmen Deli & Grocery angling to the ATM, eavesdropping on musicians as they bought cigarettes. "I'm on at Spotted Cat tonight," and "I'd like to get a new band together. I'd really like to find a singer."

I ran into the singer seeker at the relatively empty Three Muses around six, and he told me the band wouldn't go on until seven, so I ambled over to the Apple Barrel.

The Apple Barrel

COZY BOHEMIAN BAR WITH INFORMAL NEW ORLEANS JAZZ; OPEN MONDAY–THURSDAY AND SUNDAY 1 P.M. TO 3 A.M., FRIDAY AND SATURDAY 1 P.M. TO 5 A.M.

609 Frenchmen St.
New Orleans, LA
70116
(504) 949-9399

An older man in sunglasses was on the bongos, another on guitar; a third on clarinet staggered between blues, folk, and jazz as I forked over some cash (no checks, no credit cards) for a beer. The chalkboard behind them said the "Hip Shakers," but the bartender said they didn't really have a name. "Sometimes on a Sunday you don't really know who's gonna show up."

A lubricated group of vacationing Floridians fretted over the bathroom and getting change for a $20 to give something to the homeless guy outside and whether they were going to get a table at Adolfo's, the restaurant upstairs. The bartender assured them they would be OK. The bar was largely choked with out-of-towners, whereas it seemed the locals took the tables along the street window. The Apple Barrel is dimly lit and dreamily bohemian. It's a good start to the night. The band was settling into a congenial jangle when suddenly a cornet sounded from a table near the door and the bartender whispered, "That's Jack Fine!" Fine is most often associated with the Spotted Cat down the street, so I dropped a couple of bucks in the band's bucket and wandered out to see who was wailing in his place.

The Spotted Cat

QUINTESSENTIAL JAZZ CLUB WITH BANDS THAT FOCUS ON THE STAN-DARDS; OPEN WEEKDAYS 4 P.M. TO 2 A.M., WEEKENDS 3 P.M. TO 2 A.M.

623 Frenchmen St.
New Orleans, LA
70116
(206) 337-3273

The Spotted Cat was featuring Kristina Morales that night. She and her band worked through a traditional jazz set heavy on dream numbers: "Dream a Little Dream of Me," "I'll See You in My Dreams," and so on. The Spotted Cat is an inverse dream of a jazz joint, cleaned up and classy, lots of mirrors as if to allow its denizens a reflection of themselves in the New Orleans of lore. I took a spot back by the ATM (this place is also cash only) next to an African American gentleman in an impeccable suit and matching hat. I waited for a heads-up that he was also someone in the New Orleans music pantheon I should know, but instead a woman with the weirdest eyebrows I've ever seen yammered away at the bar about football as fleece-clad tourists ponied up for drinks. All the customers applauded Morales's charming delivery of songs they half knew, and more folks started to pile in. One guy with a take-out container looked around a little frantically until the bartender called to him,

"Got a spot for you at the end of the bar tonight," and poured him his drink. It's not a bad place to be a regular, but as that guy got settled, the well-coiffed gentleman suddenly animated and made for the exit, leaning on his walking stick. It was like watching a shift change.

The Three Muses

CROWDED GOURMET SMALL-PLATES RESTAURANT WITH LIVE JAZZ EVERY EVENING; OPEN EVERY DAY EXCEPT TUESDAY 4 P.M. UNTIL THE WEE HOURS; KITCHEN HOURS 5 P.M. TO 10, 11, OR 12 P.M., DEPENDING ON THE DAY

536 Frenchmen St.
New Orleans, LA
70116
(504) 298-8746
thethreemuses.com

It was (early) show time at the Three Muses and I was anxious to get a table, but all the spots were taken, so I took up residence at the corner of the bar. I envied the advance planning of a woman sitting in a coveted corner table alone, reading a book. The Three Muses has an amazing small-plates menu, and each dish that edged by complicated my order, but I held to my resolve for the lamb sliders with tomato chutney and herbed goat cheese. I was rewarded with something akin to what the gods on Olympus get when they are hungry for White Castle: two perfectly salty, rich, tangy small burgers for only $7. Three Muses takes credit cards, and I considered another dish when Linnzi Zaorski and crew (guitar, upright bass, and violin) took the bandstand. Ms. Zaorski, with jet-age curls and a clock-stopping dress, performed a set of World War II jazz from the USO show of the soul. A couple danced ostentatiously in the sole empty spot near the door.

The night's progression from somewhat gritty to relatively posh had started to take hold. I wondered if on this short

Linnzi Zaorski at the Three Muses

Kristina Morales at the Spotted Cat

stretch of Frenchmen Street one could zip back and forth across the strata of class and history. Back out on the street was a glut of hipster musicians in smart vintage suits rubbing against the rainbow of pierced street urchins. Someone tried to make an appointment with the tattooist closing up shop, but the schedule seemed shaky. A goateed cat with a swell fedora sped by on a beater bike, balancing a sax case on the handlebars. The folks on the sidewalk before me said, "Let's follow him!" As good a plan as any.

I would maintain that if you were going to be in New Orleans for only one night, Frenchmen Street will give you perhaps the juiciest taste of the city, though perhaps a bit sanitized.

Louisiana Music Factory

A ONE-STOP RECORD SHOP FOR ALL KINDS OF LOUISIANA MUSIC, PAST AND PRESENT

210 Decatur Street
New Orleans, LA
70130
(504) 586-1094
www.louisianamusic
factory.com

Whenever anyone tells me they are searching for some CD of Louisiana music, the first thing I ask is if they've called the Louisiana Music Factory in New Orleans, because if they don't have it, or don't know where to get it, chances are it doesn't exist. The record shop occupies a long, narrow storefront on Decatur Street in the French Quarter, across from the New Orleans location of the House of Blues franchise. It's easy to mistake for one of the ubiquitous New Orleans memorabilia shops that clog the Quarter, selling Mardi Gras beads and novelty T-shirts to tourists, and in fact I thought that very thing for many years.

I was looking for *Solo,* a 2006 collection of haunting minimalist pieces for saxophone and synthesizer by Cecilia, Louisiana, native Dickie Landry. Landry, currently a saxophonist for Lil' Band o' Gold, is a painter and founding member of the Philip Glass Ensemble and collaborator with Laurie Anderson, the Talking Heads, Robert Rauschenberg, Paul Simon, and about any other artist you can name, but his own recordings proved hard to find. Then and now, the Louisiana Music Factory is the first thing that comes up online when you search for this particular album, but the real shock came when I went down to New Orleans and the clerk knew exactly who I was talking about and in minutes found it in the stacks.

On that day when I found the Dickie Landry album, two different musicians came by to drop off copies of their own CDs to add to the stacks; the shop acting as much as a repository as a marketplace. Those stacks, befitting of the culture they reflect, escape the bounds of simple categorizations. Gospel records might also be R&B records, a Cajun artist might also be a country artist. The staff there understands that the stylistic lines that define most record stores are porous at best as far as Louisiana music is concerned.

The shop carries books, vinyl records, CDs, tapes, whatever media transmit the vibrations of the culture, and features a rolling calendar of in-store performances with the people that make those vibrations. In-store appearances by indie rock bands are a staple in the struggling record store industry, but I imagine there are few shops around that feature jam bands and up-and-coming jazz artists in the same week, sometimes on the same night.

The beautiful conceit of the Louisiana Music Factory is that it mirrors the Louisiana musical landscape without comment; it deals in no more and no less than Louisiana music. It has everything the tourist and the specialist are looking for and all the unexplored space in between. In many ways, the Louisiana Music Factory is a distillation of Louisiana's love of its own musical culture. The shop is content to have Louisiana music be its world, because there is always something new in that world to explore.

Hi-Ho Lounge

HIP LOCAL BAR WITH LOCAL ROCK, ROOTS, PUNK, AND WEEKLY BLUEGRASS SHOWS

2239 St. Claude
(corner of St. Claude
and Marigny)
New Orleans, LA
70117
(504) 945-4446
hiholounge.net/

From Frenchmen Street, double back a little down Rampart Street, past the spots where Donna's once was the ground zero for brass bands, where the Saenger Theatre sits in seemingly perpetual readiness to reopen, where the sketchy neighborhood around Armstrong Park is being redrawn with pricey condominiums, and you start to get back to the grit. The Hi-Ho is one of your first stops, or the last if you fear to venture any farther.

I visited some time after Hurricane Katrina and was thrilled to see it had reopened. The Hi-Ho was always one of those secondary destinations for me in my formative years going to the city. We'd catch a show at Tipitina's or the old Storyville Jazz Hall (it still rankles me that a Jimmy Buffet—themed tourist trap sits where Storyville Jazz Hall once stood) and then be on the hunt for something else. The Hi-Ho is tucked away in the St. Roch neighborhood, right past Elysian Fields as you head down St. Claude, in a funky red building. I remember there was some weird deal where you had to knock first and know a password or something before going in. It felt positively bohemian. Inside, the floors were painted a riot of colors, and freaks of all stripes were there listening to a funk band, or a punk trio, or Motown hits—you never quite knew what to expect. There was also a large cage in the corner that got put to various uses depending on the entertainment.

As I walked in on a slow Monday after JazzFest had dissipated, I spied a cleaned-up, classier version of the old place. The ceilings used to be disarmingly low, but once Katrina wreaked havoc, millworker and new owner John Hartsock went to work. "The ceiling looked like a parachute when I walked in," he says. "But when I looked in the attic, I saw the original high

New Orleans

ceiling could be salvaged." The stained cypress ceiling and bar look radiant against the rust red walls and the stained green concrete floor. The same small box stage I remember is to the back, flanked on the left by the cage. When asked about the cage's history, he chuckled, "If I had a dime for every time I heard that question, I could've financed the renovations." Hartsock has managed to revitalize the club, class it up a little without losing the charm the place has always had for me. "We have the funky dive feel, without the funky dive funk," he explains.

Like before, the club caters to a lot of different audiences. There are punk shows, funk shows, acoustic shows, but the feature that brought me down was the weekly bluegrass jam that happens every Monday night. The lynchpin to the weekly gathering is Pat Flory, who was dutifully tuning a battered vintage mandolin as I talked to him. "This instrument wasn't vintage when I got it, it just got that way along with me." Flory is the founder of the Piney Woods Opry radio program in Abita Springs, has played at JazzFest, and has an encyclopedic knowledge of the instruments and music he plays. "Country music is in my roots," he says. "My mother's uncle was the fiddler in the Mississippi Possum Hunters," he explains over the plunk of the double strings. "I've been listening to and playing country music all my life. Bluegrass is a subset of country, a honing in on it." Not wanting to split hairs, he further explains, "Country music is elastic, reflective of place and time. The high point for me was about fifty years ago, when people born on farms started moving to the city, and all the anguish that came with that. That's where Hank Williams and folks like that were coming from."

A small circle of musicians came in, and the congenial group quickly got down to the business of some high lonesome. The harmonies and interplay among this group were stellar, despite it not being a regular, rehearsing band. They pulled from a vast repertoire of country and bluegrass notables throughout the evening, and for a moment I was transported away from the city at the foothills of recovery, from the blue tarps flapping in the lazy spring evening breeze, to a place where people take their adversity in stride, where hard times become as inconsequential as the weather. The group finished "Worried Man Blues" with its message of resiliency and hope: "It takes a worried man to sing a worried song / I'm worried now but I won't be worried long." I stepped out into the perfect evening air with renewed faith in the future of a city I know and love.

King Pin Bar

HOMEY UPTOWN LOCALS BAR

1307 Lyons St.
New Orleans, LA
70115
(504) 891-2373
kingpinbar.com/

The King Pin is a scrappy little neighborhood bar that makes you wish immediately that Uptown was your neighborhood. My first time there was after a rather concentrated New Orleans afternoon—a fifth Katrina anniversary remembrance in the Ninth Ward complete with Rebirth Brass Band and dancing in the streets—and before heading back, I sought out something a little more subdued. I failed to find that at the King Pin. It was karaoke night; that scourge of the entertainment world was raging full gale in the pub, but New Orleans has a way of pushing karaoke to a new extreme while endearing it. One couple worked their way painfully through "Shout!" from the Blues Brothers. He was confident, if tuneless; she was hammered and ill equipped for the "little bit louder now's" she was assigned. I may never be able to hear that song correctly again, nor "Purple Rain" from later on in the evening, but there was a warmth one finds rarely in karaoke's cold charms.

Now this sounds like any bar anywhere, I know, and in many ways the King Pin is that proverbial "any bar." There are countless bars like it in Uptown New Orleans, where the folks are still unmistakably New Orleanian but have eschewed the boho circus act that can wear you down in the hipper parts of the city, but there is still that essence to it that sets it apart from a neighborhood joint in other parts of the country.

The owners of the King Pin as well as the bartenders took to the mic, forgoing the karaoke standards for a litany of Saints chants, namely, "Halftime (Stand Up and Get Crunk)" by the Ying Yang Twins. Like karaoke, the Ying Yang Twins are generally asinine and mindless, yet after the still

153

unbelievable 2009 Super Bowl win by the Saints, "Stand Up and Get Crunk" has become a mission statement. The bar stood up—some leaning, a few precariously balanced upon bar stools—and got crunk. The beauty in "crunkness" is twofold. The main part is an unhinged celebration for which the city is particularly apt, but it also contains a modicum of constraint, a self-consciousness that wasn't quite as pronounced before Katrina. The Super Bowl win was a magical moment, even for a non–sports fan like me. It was the opposite "Oh Shit" of the storm, the kind that makes you believe anything is possible.

The massive gravity of karaoke resumed control of the evening. Someone set into bungling a Bon Jovi tune under the watchful gaze of the velvet portraits over the bar, and the taco truck outside (Taceaux Loceaux, with recipes from a chef that studied under Emeril Lagasse, no less) announced a last call, and it was one of those simple magic nights that makes a neighborhood and a city and a life.

The Maple Leaf

TRADITIONAL NEW ORLEANS PIANO BAR WITH LIVE MUSIC MOST EVENINGS;
WALTER "WOLFMAN" WASHINGTON PERFORMS ON SUNDAY

8316 Oak St.
New Orleans, LA
70118
(504) 866-9359
mapleleafbar.com/

Farther off the beaten path in the delightfully bohemian environs of Oak Street lies the funky watering hole the Maple Leaf. It opened in 1974, one of the longest continually open bars in the city. It's the bar where Henry Butler and James Booker and countless other titans of New Orleans piano music rattled the rafters and kept the dark narrow box of a room jumping into the wee hours. It's where Walter "Wolfman" Washington held court for years and where new meets old; Rebirth Brass Band, one of the most respected of the city's brass bands, has a standing Tuesday night residency, while comparative upstart Papa Grows Funk keeps things hopping on Monday nights.

The real night to hit the Maple Leaf, though, is Sunday, when the $8 cover includes free boiled shrimp or crawfish (depending on the season) followed by the Joe Krown Trio with Walter "Wolfman" Washington and Russell Batiste. It's really about as New Orleans a thing as you can do. Washington got his start in the fifties as a guitarist in Lee Dorsey's band and then in the seventies played with soul legend Johnny Adams. Joe Krown is the king of New Orleans–style Hammond B-3 organ, having played for Clarence "Gatemouth" Brown from 1992 until Gate's passing in 2005, and in the last half of the nineties he held down the weekly Traditional Piano Night slot at the Maple Leaf. Drummer Russell Batiste got his start with Charmaine Neville's band in the mid-eighties and with the Funky Meters (the reincarnation of the original Meters from the seventies) and continues to be a catalyst for the funk side of New Orleans.

With these three, New Orleans funk

takes on a cosmic gravity, a massive entity that absorbs R&B and blues and jazz and anything else in its path. Get your fill of crawfish on a Sunday and manage enough beers from the crowded bar adjacent to the stage, and their smoothest of smooth groove will likely produce an out-of-body experience.

It's something not hard to have in the Maple Leaf. One of my favorite nights out in New Orleans was to see Mississippi bluesman T-Model Ford play with members of the house band. The night wore on, and at 3 a.m. Ford had been playing a solo riff on "Mannish Boy" for half an hour, I think. I say that because I think I faded out on the bench that lines the wall of the darkened room, but I perked up when members of the house band jumped in, and they launched into another thirty minutes of "Mannish Boy." Time suddenly became meaningless, as did the differential between songs, between blues and funk and whatever. Like any truly successful show, it had become its own space in the universe, one I'm not unconvinced continues to rattle on years later after I left, just before the first threat of dawn.

Ogden Museum of Southern Art

CONTEMPORARY AND FOLK ART MUSEUM WITH LIVE MUSIC IN THE ATRIUM ON
THURSDAY EVENINGS

925 Camp St.
New Orleans, LA 70130
(504) 539-9600
ogdenmuseum.org

Right around the corner from the Circle Bar, on Camp Street, right off Lee Circle, lies the Odgen Museum of Southern Art—a glorious temple to the reassessment of our southern identity. The boxy front of the building is softened immediately by the presence of lawn chairs in the entryway, creating an inviting front porch.

The galleries form a squared-off spiral, like a bent slinky, around a cavernous atrium, creating lofty but cozy alcoves for the art, designed for unguided wandering. My favorites were the top-floor exhibition by New Orleans folky surrealist Robert Warrens, whose bright lyrical canvases offered a poetic snapshot of the city's recovery, and lack thereof, after Katrina. I was also struck by one of the many architectural details of the building, a clear glass square set in a grid of frosted blocks on the wall facing Camp Street. It made a crystal clear snapshot of the city outside float midair like a painting. Really, it's a stunning window.

But this was Thursday evening, and my attention was undeniably drawn to Gal Holiday, singing her exquisite brand of country twang into the ether from the ground-floor lobby as a part of the Ogden's weekly After Hours concert series. One wouldn't think the tall chamber would make a good concert hall, but Holiday's sweet Patsy Cline croon soared through the building with ease. One thinks of classical country music as belonging to the world, but Gal Holiday and her band are nearly omnipresent in New Orleans and the surrounding area; her sleeve of tattoos intersecting with her immediately friendly delivery is as New Orleans as it gets.

The museum sets

Gal Holiday at the Ogden Museum of Southern Art

out a number of seats so you can gather around the stage and get an intimate view of how the music is made. Beer and wine are sold in an alcove to the back, a kids' craft table is set up at the top-floor landing, and the roof-top terrace offers a great view of the Warehouse District and the bridge, along with another cash bar. The music fills the entire building, so you really do not miss a thing as you peruse the galleries and gift shop. What these events do is dismantle the whole notion of museums as quiet, austere places, revealing them to be vibrant, noisy even, and alive.

On my second visit, the Ogden featured New Orleans Jimmy Dean True Value Country Showdown winner Christian Serpas and Ghost Town. Like Gal Holiday the week before, Serpas and crew used the natural echo in the building to their advantage as they doled out what they refer to as American Honky-Tonk music, winning over the crowd with classic country tunes and originals. I walked in as Serpas admitted to the crowd that he, like me, first heard Vince Taylor's 1958 classic "Brand New Cadillac" via The Clash; he then launched into it.

The concerts here have a decidedly educational tone to them, with the performers telling personal and historical back stories of the songs they play. In the second part of the show, WWOZ DJ Bill DeTurk leads an informal question-and-answer series with the artist, digging into the history and motivations for doing these songs and pursuing their art.

One Eyed Jack's

UNIQUE PERFORMANCE HALL WITH NATIONAL AND LOCAL ROCK, R&B, AND ROOTS MUSIC;
OPEN MONDAY–WEDNESDAY AND SUNDAY 7 P.M. TO 3 A.M., THURSDAY 5:30 P.M. TO 3 A.M.,
FRIDAY–SATURDAY 5:30 P.M. TO 5 A.M.

615 Toulouse St.
New Orleans, LA
70130
(504) 569-8361
oneeyedjacks.net

One Eyed Jack's consists of a cozy little bar on the street and a dreamlike, burlesque-themed nightclub in the back that plays host for both locals and the bohemian bands that you get the feeling would maybe like to become that. The performers run in cycles of traveling indie rock groups, local burlesque troupes, and underground rock. Then there is the New Orleans Bingo! Show, a multifaceted rock theater extravaganza that combines all of the above. It's a must-see if you are looking to get a taste of New Orleans's nascent weirdness.

My particular favorite night among many at One Eyed Jack's was when Andre Williams played with a cadre of local players. Andre is one of the original dirty old men of R&B with songs like "Jail Bait" and "Pussy Stank" and an amazing career arc that took him through Berry Gordy to Ike Turner to living under a bridge in Chicago and back to the stage. Williams was bedecked in a killer red suit, rolling through his hilarious, off-color material bookended by two go-go dancers from the city's burgeoning burlesque scene (not to be confused with the city's infamous stripper scene a few blocks over on Bourbon Street) on either side of the stage. It seemed coyly decadent, the kind of night one hopes to find in a velvet painting of a club like this.

New Orleans

Domino Sound Record Shack

MAYBE THE LAST COOL RECORD STORE AND A MICROCOSM OF NEW ORLEANS HIPSTERISM

2557 Bayou Rd.
New Orleans, LA
70119
(504) 309-0871

Part of what makes New Orleans so difficult to define—and what makes it so enthralling—is the infinite scope of the place. And one way that infinitude comes through is in the local embrace of music. "New Orleans music" means something different to every listener; it might be Dixieland or funk or bounce or ragtag street musicians or seasoned pros. It might be a quick embrace of the latest trend or a tireless clinging to one that has long gone out of favor in the rest of the world, but somehow, in the humid stew that is New Orleans, things have a curious way of becoming part of the city's fabric.

That's what I was thinking the last time I was in Domino Sound Record Shack. It's a vestige of a breed dying in the digital age—the hip record store. A vinyl-only shop, it attracts a particular set that only likes a good tune but is embroiled in the context of it. The shop is impeccably curated with its selections of punk, soul, R&B, jazz, you name it—I'm particularly drawn to the bin of Jamaican 45's and the untold treasures it holds. I was musing about where I could score a jukebox to fill with these forgotten ska and rocksteady luminaries and be happy for the rest of my days when in padded the embodiment of New Orleans's love of music, its context, and itself—the New Orleans hipster.

Too-small porkpie hat, barefoot, shorts, baby in a front sling, he announced his presence to the room with faked surprise at the new-releases rack. "Oh! You have that new Quintron record, . . ." holding it aloft so he and his child could find themselves reflected in it. The clerk acted a little surprised at his surprise. "You thought we wouldn't have it?" "Oh, I meant that I have it already. I've just never seen where anyone else had it."

And so the dance began. The hipster critiqued the selections on the display racks—were they rare enough? Did they convey a holy grail quality, quickening the record nerd's interest, or were they simply groovy decorations? With a modicum of seriousness, the hipster suggested they let him curate their display racks. The staff demurely countersuggested they did a fine job of it themselves.

This sort of cultural jockeying is commonplace in New Orleans. One can fall into a listing of someone's well-known friends and attenuated tastes without seeing it coming, and it can get tiresome except for one thing—New Orleans hipsters are serious about it. They really do know their music, their tastes are that expertly crafted, and they are the ones that maintain the city's cultural tenacity. They give each other something to strive for, and in the striving, create a great place for the rest of us.

The hipster was drowned out by the crackly funk records spun by the staff—I silently prided myself on recognizing a song by Arkansas obscurity Little Beaver—and he eventually left without purchasing anything, leaving us the benefit of his aura in the room. I made my way through the gospel section and then back to the Jamaican, picked out a King Tubby 45 even though I haven't had a working turntable in years. I suppose I just wanted to be cool enough to come back.

Preservation Hall

THE MOST TRADITIONAL JAZZ HALL ON THE PLANET WITH LIVE MUSIC EVERY NIGHT

726 St. Peters
New Orleans, LA
70116
(504) 522-2841
preservationhall.com

While much of New Orleans is awash in reinvention, in mutation and melding of styles, Preservation Hall is the eternal unchanging hub around which much of the city's music spins. The building had its start as a private residence in 1750 but became the permanent home of traditional New Orleans jazz in 1961. In keeping with the ethos of the city, the Hall is anything but formal; at 8 p.m. on any day of the week, you pile in and find a spot on the floor surrounding the band, literally sitting at the feet of masters (unless you spring for VIP seating; then you get a chair).

Clint Maedgen playing sax at Preservation Hall (Photo by Shannon Brinkman)

The house bands vary throughout the week, from the Preservation Hall Jazz Masters to the Swing Kings and Hall-Stars, but really any night will set you right. The music that goes down in the Hall is not exactly Dixieland, certainly not the spit-shine-clean version one can find in nearby tourist traps in the French Quarter, nor does it concede to the common notion of jazz. Instead, it is the deeply traditional pulse of this city, the piano- and clarinet-driven wellspring from which most of America's popular music can be derived on some level. It is the touchstone that continually feeds the city's music, and it is where the music comes back when it needs realignment. True, the Hall is mainly filled up with tourists, but it's one of the instances of the real thing that those tourists are likely to get. I mean, you never get through a Preservation Hall show without the "Saints Go Marching In" before it's over.

New

The Saturn Bar

FUNKY, GRUNGY BAR FEATURING MUSIC FROM NEW ORLEANS'S UNDERGROUND; OPEN
THURSDAY–SUNDAY 5 P.M. TO 2 A.M.

3067 St. Claude Ave.
New Orleans, LA
70117
(504) 949-7532

If the Hi-Ho is a slightly cleaned-up, grown-up version of the bohemia I remember, the Saturn Bar is the city's messy teenage bedroom of yesteryear. It's a little like being in a fevered brain—the cramped dance floor, paintings everywhere superimposed like racing thoughts, layered like a panted exhortation. It is the place to experience one of New Orleans's most interesting entities, a show by Mr. Quintron & Miss Pussycat.

Miss Pussycat at the
Saturn Bar

Mr. Quintron is an expat from Chicago who seems like he was specifically designed by cosmic forces for New Orleans. The self-styled "swamp tech" artist plays an organ fronted with a vintage car grill (cut from Ernie "Mother in Law" K-Doe's Cadillac, complete with working headlights) and his "Drumbuddy," a light-activated synthesizer that uses perforated coffee cans to dictate his rhythms, creating primitive, funky dance music that sent the sardine-packed dance floor at the Saturn Bar into a writhing frenzy. Every Quintron show starts with Miss Pussycat's bizarre puppet show, in which flowers and skeletons do battle with wolves and monsters, all on an effects budget that makes vintage Dr. Who episodes seem extravagant. The sweaty, rapt crowd cheered like Romans when the devil's head was knocked off its stick and tumbled into the pit. Once the battle concluded, Quintron was back at the organ kicking out wave after wave of intoxicating minimalist funk. At one point, Miss Pussycat and Maraccula, a synchronized maracashaking dance troupe, surrounded Quintron, who had lost his shirt in the heat, shouting out the call-and-response crowd favorite "Swamp Buggy Bad Ass," sending the dance floor into overdrive. It made an improbable, even ridiculous scene: just another night in New Orleans.

Tipitina's

TRADITIONAL LIVE-MUSIC VENUE FOR LOCAL BRASS BANDS AND FUNK AND
TOURING ROCK BANDS

501 Napoleon Ave.
New Orleans, LA
70115
(504) 895-TIPS
tipitinas.com/

My musical upbringing largely took place under the watchful eye of the Professor Longhair statue that greets you at the entrance of Tipitina's, though truthfully, that upbringing didn't really involve all that much New Orleans music. The midsize, ramshackle club opened in 1977 as a place for Fess (aka Henry Roeland Byrd) to play during his final years and thus bears the name of one of the pianist's most famous songs, but the regional alternative and punk bands that would play there were the draw for this listener in the late eighties. A glance at the calendar now will show the tide has turned a little, that the new big names in New Orleans music take up the stage most nights.

It's part of the bellwether change that took place after Katrina. It seemed the first people back in town were the restaurateurs, then the brass bands, and it has instilled a new reverence in the city for its own music. New Orleans has always had a healthy love for itself, but often the brass bands were relegated to tourist stops and a network of lesser-known clubs throughout the city. Now, they are granted the big stages.

It's a rather fortuitous thing, given that Tip's is a great place to see a band. The stage rises high enough off the packed floor that any average-height human being can get a good view, and the balcony offers a perfect perch from which to dangle your beer and watch the mayhem in relative peace.

Bruce Daigrepont has hosted his Cajun fais-do-do there every Sunday evening since time immemorial, one of the strongest links to the greater Cajun community outside New Orleans, but the thing to see here is the brass. One night,

Drive-by Truckers at Tipitina's

I was at Tip's for a private event featuring entertainment by the Dynamites, a Nashville-based well-oiled soul armada fronted by the peerless Charles Walker, who had his start opening for Wilson Pickett and James Brown at the Apollo. In other words, not a bad band to have play your event, but afterward the Soul Rebels Brass Band took over and it was a whole different ball game.

Soul Rebels are a relatively young crew who got their big break opening up for the Neville Brothers at Tipitina's. They do the parade music, the second-line and jazz funeral anthems, but they also inject their sound with R&B, funk, and hip-hop, sometimes all at once, allowing listeners to tap into whatever strain of music they like. In many ways, they embody the reality of New Orleans music, in that there are no finely etched lines between the various styles of music that fill the night air. All I know is that all networking and hobnobbing at this particular event came to a screeching halt and everyone was on the dance floor as the Soul Rebels worked the brass funk continuum to death. New Orleans is like that; sometimes you don't know what you are paying attention to, but you are nonetheless riveted.

Vaughn's Lounge

TRADITIONAL BAR WITH LIVE R&B BY KERMIT RUFFINS ON THURSDAY NIGHTS

4229 Dauphine St.
New Orleans, LA
(504) 947-5562

Before Katrina, I'd never been to one of Vaughn's Thursday nights—where there's free gumbo and Kermit Ruffins fronts his band, the Barbeque Swingers—mainly because it was one of those events that is so New Orleans that you assume it will be around forever, and then suddenly it seemed like all those things were forever lost.

On my first trip back to post-Katrina New Orleans, many of the buildings looked like they'd been freshly ravished by nature. I met up with some old friends at the venerable watering hole, and they spoke with similar shock of having their world ripped asunder. New Orleans people, the ones who really live and breathe the city, aren't exactly suited to live elsewhere. The slow, divey circadian rhythms of Thursdays at Vaughn's, Sundays at the Maple Leaf, and so on are integral to their psychic clockwork of the city. Without them, New Orleans would cease being itself.

Ruffins's Thursday night at Vaughn's was one of the first things that came back online after Katrina and, thanks to its prominence in the early episodes of HBO's New Orleans character study *Tremé,* has come to represent the city's resilient charm. Kermit still barbeques out front before the show and occasionally on stage during the show, and his complex, glorious mix of blues, R&B, and funk all laced with a little Latin swagger still establishes this hole-in-the-wall as—every Thursday anyway—the center of the universe. With so many iconic clubs having fallen off the map in recent years—the Funky Butt, Donna's, the Mother in Law Lounge, and so on—one hopes Ruffins will keep the grill fired up for years to come.

New Orleans

Birdie's Roadhouse

CLASSIC ROADHOUSE BAR WITH LIVE BLUES, FOLK, AND CAJUN MUSIC

26646 North Hwy. 21
Varnado, LA
70426
(985) 732-4032
myspace.com/
birdiesbigsound

The American South is a truly fertile environment. Weeds and flowers and people and music all grow with wild gusto in the soil here, even in places that seem completely untended. My latest find on this journey through the wild gardens of our culture is Birdie's Roadhouse, nine miles north of Bogalusa on Highway 21. I don't really make it out to Bogalusa or tiny outskirt community Varnado very often. Not a dig against the area; it is just off my usual routes. Of course, that's where the great stuff grows.

Birdie's is a smallish, one-room cypress building on the right side of the road, past the prison. It started when partners Sandy Nauman and Sam Manlove left their careers of bartending and decided to open this bar. "Sam was going to retire and we decided we didn't like any of the bars in Bogalusa, so we opened this place," explains Nauman over a bowl of spicy boiled peanuts on the club's back porch. Over my right shoulder sits a piano that used to be in the famed Studio in the Country in Bogalusa. Stevie Wonder and Willie Nelson, among countless others who have recorded there, have used that piano, and maybe some of the aura of that instrument has carried over to its new home, since Birdie's Roadhouse has perhaps the best sound of any club I have ever heard. Nauman explains that because of the exposed roof and the cypress wall and floor, the sound doesn't echo; it flows through the building.

I say it's because of the great vibe of the staff and clientele. Steven Orr, a director for Habitat for Humanity from Kansas, who is on his third visit to Birdie's, exclaimed, "This place is great! Every walk of life comes in here, and they all hug each other like family." I was sold on that when I was offered the best pot roast sandwich I've ever eaten. Manlove confided,

Varnado

"I drop in a whole jar of pepperoncinis and a can of beer in the crock pot and let it go over night." It made my whole head tingle.

To say the evening's performer, Brady Roberts, is a virtuoso on the acoustic guitar is giving credence to the soul he puts forth in his songs. His set was a mix of brilliant, intricate renditions of bar favorites and lethal slide guitar blues. When he took to the slide, the whole place started jumping. The stomping was so fierce that it actually sloshed the beer out of my glass. Roberts's version of Stevie Wonder's "Superstitious" is the most jaw-dropping acoustic guitar performance I have ever witnessed, simultaneously keeping that song's effervescent funk bass line, melody, singing, and harmonica runs—the man is a machine.

That's the beauty of this club. It resonates just like a guitar, getting the gumbo of lawyers and contractors and artists and hunters who go there to kick their shoes off and take over the dance floor. In the middle of the bar is a tall metal pole that provides the central support for the small building, but when things start hopping and the liquid courage sets in, the patrons shimmy up the pole to touch the rafters and, if chalk is handy, scrawl their name. The walls are covered with a constellation of players who have performed in the club over its six years: Henry Gray, J. Monque'D, Grayson Capps, Rockin' Jake, and countless others. "Clarence 'Gatemouth' Brown has spent his last two Christmas Eves here. He just loved the place," says Manlove.

The house band is the Petty Bones, a killer bluegrass outfit that hosts the club's Thursday open mic night. Manlove admits, "Last time we had seventeen top-notch musicians lined up to play." But I can see why. This place is so perfect that you think you are making it up. As music gets more pasteurized, as venerable night spots slowly get replaced by chains and we start spending more nights shackled to those home theater systems that cost a second mortgage, the opportunities to hear great homegrown music in a homegrown place are dwindling. The bar business is a rough one under the best circumstances, but Sam and Sandy aren't in this for the money. "It's all about the music," explains Nauman. "It's to keep the music alive." So next time you are lamenting that there is nothing to do in town, head up Highway 21 and stop at a little place that is bouncing off its foundation and rekindle your love of southern culture.

Old Firemen's Hall

MASSIVE DANCE HALL WITH LIVE SWAMP POP BANDS ON SATURDAY NIGHTS

307 Fourth St.
Westwego, LA
70094
(504) 371-0776
oldfiremenshall.com/

No one wants to go to the West Bank, or at least that's what the average New Orleanian would have you think. So shunned is the community across the river that, despite being in and around New Orleans all my life, I wasn't completely sure where Westwego was. I knew it was across the shockingly narrow Huey P. Long Bridge from New Orleans, and that as a kid we would pass through it coming from Houma into the city, but that is all I knew. I rode up with Jeffrey, a photographer now living in New Orleans, who said he mentioned to a friend that he was heading out to Westwego and that friend remarked, "Why? If the West Bank is the red-headed stepchild of New Orleans, Westwego is that child's awkward friend." True, the big box strips on Highway 90 and the vast oil storage fields dotting the river may not be able to compete with St. Charles Avenue for charm or Frenchmen Street for bohemian chic, but a visit to the weekend swamp pop concerts at the Old Firemen's Hall holds its own rewards.

The Old Firemen's Hall has been a central fixture in West-wego since 1919 and has been operating as a dance hall since swamp pop began. Rob Billiot took over managing the club in 2006, when it was threatened with demolition to make room for houses on Fourth Street. Billiot's parents—his dad, Robert, the mayor of Westwego; and his mother, Pamela, the principal of the elementary school across the street—collected enough money to save the building and refurbish it after it was ravaged by Katrina. Rob teaches business classes at Archbishop Shaw High School across the river, and his parents asked him to be the manager.

Rob loves his clientele and how his club has factored into

Westwego

their lives. "Some of the guys used to come here when this placed first opened as a dance hall in the sixties," explains Rob. "They used to pay a nickel at the door. Every week I have someone tell me they met their wife at dances here." Like other venues like this, the Old Firemen's Hall is as much a community center as it is a nightclub. When we walk in, a group of young men stalk the pool tables with predatory concern, while a few tables away a family is celebrating a birthday party. The bar is lined with thirty-year-olds, while a couple of grandmas jump up to dance when a song from their youth comes from the bandstand.

The dance floor dominates the room, and the band for this evening's jam, largely pulled from the roster of swamp pop powerhouse Foret Tradition, summons all dancers to their feet. I love that people dance in Louisiana; it is among our most redeeming qualities. Two generations of couples hit the floor when the band kicked into "Don't Close the Door on Me." The floor ebbed and flowed in capacity until a line dance broke out to "Don't Tease Me." I'm glad to see line dancing is alive and well, even though I am personally terrible at it. The movement in unison, that understanding of the steps, that willingness to not only get out there but hang in there with the rest of them is, to me, endemic of what is beautiful about Louisiana culture.

Swamp pop is not the only long-forgotten dance ritual that has found a new lease on life at the Old Firemen's Hall. Wednesday night is Jamaican dance club night. It has nothing to do with reggae or dance hall or even the country. The Jamaica, originating at the old Irish Channel dance hall the Jamaica Club in the 1950s, is a highly stylized Lindy Hop that has steps with names like the "Roy Close" and the "Des Allemands." It's a curious throwback to a simpler time, much like swamp pop and the sweet mix of people at the Old Firemen's Hall.

EPILOGUE

Mid City Lanes Rock 'n' Bowl

BOWLING ALLEY AND NEW ORLEANS INSTITUTION THAT UNDERSCORES NEW ORLEANS'S COMMITMENT TO ITS CULTURE

3000 South
Carrollton Ave.
New Orleans, LA
70118
(504) 861-1700
www.rocknbowl.com

Perhaps no place represents the push-and-pull of New Orleans better than the Rock 'n' Bowl. Once upon a time it was simply Mid City Lanes, a classic bowling alley on the second floor of an unremarkable shopping center at the corner of Tulane and Carrollton avenues, just off the ramp of U.S. 61, where the fabled blues highway made its slow descent to its southern terminus at Carondelet Street. In the early nineties, the owner, John Blancher, got the bright idea to start hosting zydeco bands on Thursday nights after the leagues finished their sets. The dance floor was cramped, awkward even, confronting you the instant you made it up the steps with the low stage off to one side, the bar to the other. You had to wade into the sweaty throng of zydeco-hungry dancers to get a drink or to get a late-night frame in. The band would enter and exit the stage through the service lane, the same one the alley attendants would use to free a ball stuck in the return mechanism or a pin jammed in the setters. It was a preposterous and magnificent place to see some music.

In 1995 a *National Geographic* story let the world know New Orleans's best-kept secret, and soon the Rock 'n' Bowl became a totem of New Orleans, a link between greater American culture—what is more American than a bowling alley?—and the curiosity of zydeco. Cajun, blues, swamp pop, rock 'n' roll, and variety bands soon filled the calendar four or five nights a week. You didn't go there

to bowl, or I never did anyway; you went there for the music. Climbing those steps into that divey relic of a place was like ascending the mountain of American music, a peak at the end of the blues highway where you could get a long view of how far Louisiana culture had spread.

Then came Katrina. The building was largely trashed, and though the alley was upstairs, it seemed that, like the rest of New Orleans, and much of Louisiana by extension, it was washed into history. Who would reopen a wrecked bowling alley with a cramped dance floor, a place that seemed like a haphazard idea to begin with?

Louisianians would. Blancher called in favors with the power company, the newspaper, and the community, and hired New Orleans R&B legend Eddie Bo to play on reopening night: November 10, 2005. It seemed the only light in the city was that neon bowling pin out front. It seemed that the same bizarre will that created the Rock 'n' Bowl in the first place would be the seed for New Orleans's regeneration.

The problem was that we are talking New Orleans here, a place that didn't function like clockwork in the best of situations, and the Rock 'n' Bowl struggled along as the only tenant in the shopping center for two years until the center was sold and the Blancher started looking for a new location.

Fortunately, Blancher also owned Ye Olde College Inn just a few blocks down Carrollton, and in April 2009, a newer, better Rock 'n' Bowl rose in the restaurant's parking lot. The setup is eerily the same, except it's all on the ground floor and double the size. The stage is to the right, the bar to the left, and you still enter through the dance floor, a string of state-of-the-art lanes lining the back. Compared to its cramped, dimly lit predecessor, this Rock 'n' Bowl is a luminous cathedral.

On opening night, dancers dotted the massive dance floor as the reigning king of New Orleans music, Kermit Ruffins and his Barbecue Swingers, held court from the well-appointed stage. They did New Orleans by the numbers, "Iko Iko," "The

Saints Come Marching In," and a new standard, the theme from HBO's *Tremé.* A guest vocalist got up and sent "Try a Little Tenderness," even pulling the college girls lounging in what looked like a conference room behind the bar to the floor. It was fantastic.

Tourist families herded kids around like it was a Disneyland attraction, and in some ways it is. The crowd got the most excited when Ruffins and crew launched into the Black Eyed Peas' omnipresent hit "Tonight's Gonna Be a Good Night"—no better song in the world to underscore a fun but unremarkable evening. Patrons got up and danced on the stage; one freckle-faced eight-year-old sat at the edge of the stage nursing a fountain drink. Ruffins, trading on his well-deserved fame from *Tremé,* mugged for photos during the breaks when he wasn't singing or playing. At one point during "Good Night" hula hoops were distributed to the crowd, and, ever the trooper, Blancher stood on the bar and demonstrated his prowess. He was like an atomic model, a nucleus orbited by an electron.

It's an apt metaphor; the reopening of the Rock 'n' Bowl was instrumental in the reopening of the rest of New Orleans, and the shiny new location is a prime example of the adaptability that Louisiana culture will have to attain to survive. Sure, it's not the old gritty Rock 'n' Bowl—it's actually really nice in there—and anyway, how are you to create a rundown bowling alley from scratch? You could take a shabby-chic route and apply a rustic patina, lots of kitsch to imply the past; some places do that. Should a place run itself into the ground by refusing to adapt? Do we cherish the memories of a passing culture, or do we roll with what that culture has become?

Only time will tell if the Rock 'n' Bowl, and New Orleans, and Louisiana in general, can gain back some of that special hangdog patina that makes it so special a place. It's unclear whether that very patina that we think defines Louisiana even applies anymore. We want to think our rundown juke joints, our plank-floored dance halls, our rough-and-tumble honky-tonks are a necessary part of our identity, and maybe they are, but that thought must be tempered with the realization that it is a tricky balance keeping the future in check with the past. The only way to keep the two threaded together is to be a part of it—embrace the curiosities of Louisiana culture while acquiescing to the realities of the passage of time. A culture is a living thing, and it is our job to live it.

INDEX